# Encouragement
## How to Be and Find the Best

# Encouragement
## How to Be and Find the Best

Cathy Burnham Martin

Quiet Thunder Publishing
Manchester, NH    Columbus, NC    Naples, FL

QUIET THUNDER PUBLISHING

www.QTPublishing.com

This title and more are also featured at
**www.GoodLiving123.com**

# Encouragement
## How to Be and Find the Best

Paperback edition:  ISBN 978-1-939220-47-9
eBook edition:  ISBN 978-1-939220-48-6
Audiobook edition:  ISBN 978-1-939220-46-2

Published and printed in the United States of America.

Library of Congress Control Number:
2019930211

## Dedication

With the greatest admiration and love, I dedicate this book to my parents, Bob and Glenna Burnham.

There was never a day when Mom and Dad failed to encourage my siblings and me. Even when we lacked confidence and belief that we could accomplish one thing or another, they steadfastly assured us, "Of course, you can!"

If we protested, "But I tried," their retort was consistent.

"Try harder."

They worked hard without complaining. They loved without judgment. They gave without restraint. They forgave without resentment. They taught us to follow in their footsteps.

We lost my Dad on October 6, 2018. He and Mom had been married for 68 years and together for more than 70. Mom is strong and carries on their legacy. They were best friends. Lovers. Champions. Encouragers.

Thank you... and God bless you as you have so richly blessed everyone who has ever known you.

Glenna and Bob Burnham at their 65th Wedding Anniversary party in Palm Harbor, Florida.

# Table of Contents

Cover photo courtesy of Lucie Dawson

## Other Titles
**From Cathy Burnham Martin**

The Bimbo Has Brains… and Other Freaky Facts

The Bimbo Has MORE Brains… Surviving Political Correctness

A Dangerous Book for Dogs: Train Your Humans

Dog Days in the Life of the Miles-Mannered Man

Healthy Thinking Habits:  Seven Attitude Skills Simplified

Of the Same Blood:  Your Eurasian Heritage

Sage, Thyme & Other Life Seasonings:  Perspectives

Fifty Years of Fabulous Family Favorites, Volumes 1-3

Champagne!  Facts, Fizz, Food & Fun

Dockside Dining:  Round One

Dockside Dining:  A Second Helping

Dockside Dining:  Back for Thirds

Cranberry Cooking

Lobacious Lobster

The Communication Coach:
Business Communication Tips from the Pros

**To see all books and audiobooks from Cathy Burnham Martin**
**go to www.GoodLiving123.com**

## About Rust Busters

What could be better than growing into greater happiness and success, personally and professionally? Taking as many people as possible with us!

In my articles on the GoodLiving123.com website I often emphasize that we should strive to live with as much contagious enthusiasm as possible. Encouragement works the same way.

This book comes packed with instantly usable tips, tools, and secrets to unleash the Encourager that lives in each of us, identify Encouragers so we can surround ourselves with positive energy, and thrive despite the inevitable Discouragers in our midst. Read this book for amusement or personal growth or both. Read it to help someone else who may need encouragement, perhaps desperately. Read it to polish up some good living skills that may have become a bit rusty.

**Whether we are raising children, working with employees or a sales force, teaching students, serving the public, or championing any team, we benefit when we learn to be more encouraging and to surround ourselves with Encouragers.**

During our time on this planet, various people move in and out of our lives. Some are with us for relatively short periods. Others may be with us for years. Some drift in and out during various Life phases, both personal and professional. When we are more fortunate, a goodly number of these people are what we call Encouragers.

They are the ones who may call out from the sidelines, "You can do it!" Or they may stand quietly in front of us and look us in the eyes, as they calmly infirm, "You've got this."

They boost, they cheer, they support. They believe, they assist, they teach.

We are all different with different needs. Encouragers are like that, too. But each, in their own ways, have the compassion and generosity of spirit, to sincerely encourage others to do and be their best. Their approach may or may not reflect "our style." Yet, their hearts and souls sing out with the best... for *our* benefit.

They share their spirit, their time, and their talents to help others survive, achieve, and thrive. They help others build skill sets, focus on a target, attain goals, and be better people.

Of course, this is an ongoing process. We never really "arrive," but we can and should feel confident enough to take ourselves on as worthy projects.

It helps to recognize the Encouragers in our midst and draw them closer. We don't want to let these people "slip through out fingers," so to speak. From this, we all gain strength. Remember the solidarity in a stack of pencils versus one pencil. We can easily snap a single pencil in half. With a bunch of pencils, fragility vanishes. Encouragers build our strength in much the same way. Every word of encouragement adds another pencil to our arsenal.

## Then there are the Discouragers.

These folks seem focused on being the nay-sayers. They "know" all the reasons something *can't* be done, why we do not have a chance, why our plan will ultimately fail. They assuredly stack the odds and facts against us. They diminish our confidence.

With every word and look of discouragement, they take pencils away from our stack. They make us more fragile.

What is most frustrating about a Discourager? They often tend to erroneously *think* they are Encouragers. They frequently try to correct us and tell us why we should do things their way.

Throughout the book, we'll identify some common traits, styles, and behaviors of both. I think you'll recognize both.

## Most of us have a little Encourager and Discourager in us.

Once we clearly recognize the behaviors, thoughts, and processes that make us one or the other, we gain tremendous personal power. We can become more positive, more successful, more encouraging. We can also learn to surround ourselves with people who tend to be more encouraging.

Life is not always easy. It comes packed with ups and downs, turmoil, and challenges. When we are better prepared, we can meet and face the woes with greater grace, courage, and terrific tools to overcome.

We can rediscover the natural confidence, self-esteem, and poise with which we were born. We can achieve greater goals; we can genuinely feel better about ourselves, our lives, and our futures. And perhaps, most importantly, we can take other people along with us to find or rediscover their own "happy place," their greater success, their ability to positively blossom.

Does all this truly matter? I believe it does, and in an enormous way, if we want to lead happier, more fulfilling lives. We can all overcome discouragements. We all deserve encouragement.

We all know Encouragers. We all know Discouragers.

We can all grow to be more encouraged and more encouraging. We can all learn to avoid, dismiss, or deal with discouragement and Discouragers.

If you've ever faced a time when your choices, your path, your circumstances, or your life felt chaotic, out of control, pointless, or even hopeless, get ready now to find the tools you can use to not feel so low again.

We can't always control our circumstances. Life can hit us in some devastating ways. But we can do better. We can feel better. We can bounce back more quickly. We can grow in strength and ability. We can become the people we were meant to be.

Too many people struggle with discouragement. They need a little encouragement… perhaps just a few sincerely thoughtful words. They need a little shot of confidence. A boost. We can all help.

As a business speaker, I got dubbed "The Morale Booster" in a long-forgotten 1995 write-up. Initially, I didn't recognize the value of such a perception by people. It didn't seem to matter the theme or topic that had been requested for the audience. I'd hear it again and again.

"You're such a morale booster." After a keynote, graduation address, presentation, or workshop, I was overwhelmed by people expressing how much they'd "needed me" that day. How great I'd made them feel. How good it felt to feel good about themselves, their lives, and their future.

Gratitude is very encouraging. More importantly, encouragement is very morale boosting.

Now I challenge all of us to become Morale Boosters. You can use this book to become a Morale Booster Extraordinaire, or MBE. This can be used as a core course of study to earn your MBE. But, relax. There will be no quizzes, exams, or grades. This is a program for our hearts and souls.

I also believe, it's a designation we should strive to earn every single year. Remember, if I earned some degree in a traditional course of study in 1970, you could rightly wonder if I'd even have a clue about the topic in 2020, a full half century later.

The way we live our lives is hardly any different. We learn a great many skills that we continue to hone for the rest of our lives. Other skills may not get frequently used, and they tend to get rusty.

We need stay rusty no more. We can do better. We can bounce back more quickly. We can grow in strength and ability.

We have *"Encouragement... How to Be and Find the Best."* And it's loaded with glorious "Rust Busters" to help us find and appreciate Encouragers and become the Encouragers *we* are meant to be.

Happier. Fulfilled. Thriving. Empowered.

Let's journey together now. Let's grow. Let's find and be the best. Let's bust some rust!

YOU CAN !!!

Rust Buster #1
## How It All Begins

We humans feel better when we are filled with courage or strength of purpose. When our confidence is boosted, we land on top of the world!

This certainty starts as infants. An adult may whisper, "Good baby." The baby coos and cuddles comfortably.

Then we thrive on more praise for achievements as we learn words, how to feed ourselves, and develop bathroom skills. Or we falter, because praise is withheld. Many children do not receive praise for their achievements, never mind their sincere efforts.

We all need someone to assure us that our honest effort is what matters. When we make a step forward, it helps to hear that our progress is recognized, no matter how small the step may have been.

*You will never do anything in this world without courage.*
*It is the greatest quality in the mind next to honor.*
--Aristotle 384-322 BC
Greek Philosopher

Receiving sincere praise increases our motivation, especially as small children. This is most effective when the praise is very specific and recognizes true efforts and positive steps.

We learn early that when someone is an Encourager, we can bear our hearts, souls, fears, and goals with them. There is no fear that they'll slam us, laugh at us, scoff, or get angry. They won't walk out. They won't turn our vulnerabilities against us.

An Encourager doesn't try to diminish the validity of someone else's feelings just because they aren't comfortable with that someone's position. To do so would only make people feel off balance, and it gives them reason not to trust.

Encouragers don't react with impatience or overwrought emotion. They don't treat us as irrelevant or unworthy, whether we are children or adults.

We can improve our relationships with others by leaps and bounds if we become Encouragers instead of critics. We learn this as children, as we naturally gravitate to people who encourage us, without even having such awareness. This has a lot to do with how children grow and fit in with peers.

We all likely recall some children seeming to be confident, successful at anything they tried to do, magnetically attracting achievement. Other children may have appeared to drift, to not quite fit in, or to not possess pride in doing well or achieving. They may seem to slip through the cracks in society, school, or social circles.

## Most of us endure various periods of self-doubt.

These were often instilled in our youth. Sadly, they may have gotten re-enforced as we grew. As adults, we can and need to unlearn the negative from our past. Only then can we re-attain the natural grace and confidence we had at the beginning of our lives.

This process, in its entirety, is easier said than done. But we *can* do it with far less difficulty than we imagine. It starts now.

Rust Buster #1 is simple. Recognize that we were born with confidence. We were born to be Encouragers. What we unlearned, we can easily relearn. Sweet.

**Tip:** Marie Curie, the Polish-French physicist who became the first woman to win a Nobel Prize, expressed it well when she said, "Life is not easy for any of us. But what of that? We must have perseverance and above all confidence in ourselves. We must believe that we are gifted for something and that this thing must be attained."

You were born *** TO BE *** REAL ** NOT TO BE ** PERFECT

Rust Buster #2
# Identify Encouragers

*Life belongs to optimists.  Pessimists are just viewers.*

If we all were being encouraged and encouraging others, the world would be a far more beautiful place.  Just imagine!

Encouragement strengthens us and our confidence.  Encouragers help us keep on a positive track toward our goals.  Encouragers believe in our unstoppable resolve, recognize our potential, and exude an attitude of gratitude.

Encouragers don't make threats or get in an emotional rage.  They do make themselves clear.  When they say something, they mean it, but they exude compassion, especially when talking with someone whose opinions display polar opposite positions.

Regardless of our gender, our cultural background, our global location, or even our connections, we can all be Encouragers.  Naturally, there are indicators.

Some studies suggest that women may have an easier time being Encouragers.  Women tend to be raised to be nourishing and supportive.  Men are often raised to be tough and strong, and not emotionally empathetic.  Not all women and not all men fit any such stereotypes.  These are just typical findings.

Cultural variations show that certain cultures support individual efforts to encourage others.  Some cultures, unfortunately, frown on positive encouragement and support, relying instead on manipulation, terror, and power plays.

Who we develop as our personal and professional connections also plays a big role. Sometimes we choose positive, supportive friends. Sometimes, especially when we are young, we may slide a bit off track, gravitating toward people who may not set good examples, never mind be Encouragers.

To try and help me be aware of the people with whom I made friends, I remember my Dad making analogies like, "If you roll around with pigs, you will likely get muddy."

**On the other hand, he'd also say things like, "If you reach for the stars, you may not touch them, but you won't come up with a fistful of dirt either."**

My parents blessed me with directives to think, to be aware of my choices and their repercussions. They were always trying to teach me *how* to think, rather than *what* to think.

I consider those lessons as I spell out Rust Buster #2. To identify Encouragers, we are best served when we surround ourselves with people who:
1. listen and genuinely want to hear our opinions
2. react to us with positive facial expressions to urge us forward
3. share ideas and concepts that could help us
4. pave our path to make our journey easier
5. provide stepping stones and building blocks
6. offer assistance when feasible
7. help us prioritize, so we can get more things done
8. speak hopeful, helpful words
9. turn mountains into molehills
10. express as "can do" thinkers
11. lead by example
12. make and honor commitments and believe in keeping promises

13. see, appreciate, and bolster talents, skills, and strengths of others
14. help us recognize the goodness in others

Obviously, lists like this could go on for many pages. The bottom line is that encouraging people seem to effortlessly go above and beyond standard expectations. They live positive, productive lives and encourage us to do the same.

Encouragers don't blame favoritism or partisanship for any failures. They take responsibility for weaknesses or missteps and seek the lessons that can be learned to do better.

Sometimes, when we humans are struggling, we may find it easier to encourage someone else, even at times when we do not feel so positive about ourselves. We can still pay it forward. We can still give without thought of what we may get. For many of us, it takes a great deal of time and wisdom just to feel worthy. Yet, we see others as being worthy.

Interestingly, however, when we give support to others, we are inevitably encouraging them and ourselves. We are growing confidence. We are building hope. These are very empowering activities, which, in turn, reflect encouragement.

Encouragers build an internal and external support network for us. This is positively powerful. Encouragers aren't there to judge, but to lift. They help us recognize that all bad that is perpetrated against us is not a reflection on us or our value. By their actions, words, and hearts, Encouragers cause each of us to also want to be an Encourager.


**Tip:** *A friend by your side can keep you warmer than the most expensive coat.*

Rust Buster #3
## Avoid Discouragers

I love opening with a quotation, and I have two for you here. Both are by the brilliantly philosophical beast we call Anonymous.

*It is not the mountain we conquer but ourselves.*

*People who do not value you, do not deserve you.*

Just as we spoke of some basic traits of Encouragers, there are some easily recognizable signs that someone is a Discourager. Discouragers are apt to be what we call toxic people, and they display multiple negative tendencies. They tend to be people who:

- talk "at" you
- genuinely want *you* to hear *their* opinions
- scowl or look annoyed when you speak (often because they want to be speaking)
- share lots of reasons and statistics to point out why you will likely fail
- block your path to thwart your efforts
- provide obstacles and pitfalls
- offer resistance whenever possible
- set priorities so you will do what *they* want done
- speak scoffing words or give The Silent Treatment to show their disdain or to punish you
- turn molehills into mountains
- express as "can't do" thinkers

**Discouragers see the gloom in every room, the cloud on every silver lining, and the problem in front of every solution.**

We see this on Facebook or other facets of social media. Someone expresses discouragement over someone ranting at them or putting them down, trying to make them feel bad about themselves or some belief. Well, we must never give up on ourselves. Remember, we only fail when we stop trying.

*I am not discouraged,*
*because every wrong attempt discarded is another step forward.*
-- Thomas A. Edison  (1847 – 1931)
American Inventor and Businessman

Life often calls for what I call Survive and Thrive Tips. So, let's examine a few.

**Tip #1**: We must be prepared and on guard for conversation stoppers. They are not always as direct as saying something like, "Just don't talk" or even "Shut up." There are oodles of off-handed quips and lines that get the point across that they do not like your topic, do not want to hear what you are saying, or simply don't want to listen to you.

We've all heard them. They may say discouraging things like, "Whatever" or "I don't know what you want me to say," or "That's just the way it is." They may say off-putting things like, "You're going to hate me for saying this, but….," or "No offense, but…," or "I don't want to hear about this anymore."

They may say know-it-all things like, "I know I've said this before, but...," "If you were smart, you'd...," or "You know what you should have done?" They may make comments that indicate their lack of interest in listening to you, like "Agree to disagree," or "Listen, you need to relax," or the ever-popular "Just stop." They may even say condescending things, such as, "I remember going through that phase," or "Nothing personal, but...," or even "Those are *your* facts." Discouragers have an insensitive knack of making us feel like a dumb ass.

Survive and Thrive **Tip #2** says that we must listen to our hearts and tune out the negative. Compassionately consider the source, even if it is a loved one. If the discouraging words are spewing, this is someone to not take seriously, at least not on that topic. Period.

> *No one can make you feel inferior without your consent.*
> -- Eleanor Roosevelt (1884 – 1962)
> United States First Lady
> American Diplomat and Activist

**Tip #3** notes that negative people don't want someone else to feel positive. Pity parties seek more attendees. Reject those invitations. We'll have more on this later, because it is worthy of repeating and expanding.

Survive and Thrive **Tip #4** is to try to understand the reasons "why" some people become discouragers. They sometimes feel threatened by you, your success, or beliefs that you hold. They may or may not feel jealous of you, your popularity, or some attention they do not like that you received or that they felt they did not receive.

They may simply not like you. Thus, they try to do or say anything that will undercut you. They may merely lack confidence, and they make vain attempts to put others down with the delusion that it will somehow make them feel better. They may literally lack facts and information that would give them a far clearer picture of this pie called Life or, at least, your slice of it.

**Tip #5** is to learn to not worry so much about the naysayers. However, we do need to recognize them and their various symptoms. When we recognize their issues, we have an easier time not taking their put-downs to heart. We also shield ourselves against "catching" their symptoms. Negativity can be highly contagious.

Discouragers come into all our lives, usually when we least need them. Not that there is ever a great time for discouragement, but it does seem that when we are weak and most susceptible, Discouragers smell our vulnerability and pounce.

When I made the decision to become an author, I had many Encouragers. But, as with compliments and criticisms, the Discourager stands out. A person whom I believed would be one of my greatest cheerleaders, took every opportunity to spout statistics about the millions of books written each year and how virtually all authors fail to even get published, never mind become successful. Oh, joy.

Thankfully, I was not at a crossroads for which I was unprepared. I felt confident in my decision, despite the total lack of income such a move would bring. Patience and confidence often go hand-in-hand. Discouragers are not prepared for "push-back." Hah!

So, who are these Discouragers anyway, and how can we recognize them by their behavior?

We all know them. They're the folks who regularly see the glass as half empty, and they do not want anyone else to get one that's half full.

They're the "downers" who can dull the shine on a brand-new copper penny.

They're the friends who regularly try to talk us out of things we want to do. On the other hand, of course, they typically make automatic presumptions that we will be a supportive person for things *they* want to do.

Discouragers put down our opinions as poorly thought out or otherwise not viable or even interesting to consider.

## They can cause us to feel hopeless about something... or even many somethings.

They firmly and regularly try to establish priorities for us as individuals. They are intentionally or unintentionally being manipulative in reining us in to help them achieve *their* priorities, without regard nor respect for us, our priorities, or our time.

They may put down our dreams or scoff at our sincere efforts to reach for goals. They try to step on our confidence, and readily suck the wind out of our sails. These are the folks who belittle our attempts to better ourselves, either through reading and research, seeking counseling, or even working toward a higher education.

Discouragers are notorious for placing large and small roadblocks in our paths. They manage to do this even when our endeavors are positive and selfless.

For example, let's say you are studying for a test or working on an important assignment. They manage to come up with a stream of reasons why there are other things you *should* be doing. And they are likely ticked off that you didn't see that in the first place.

They may berate you in private or in public... or use humor at your expense or at the expense of a spouse, with or without the implication that they suffer from this "comic" malady. Many of us have endured such put-downs, but I most assuredly would not recommend it.

**We tend to learn from bad examples, but we should take care not to use bad examples as a rationalization of our own bad behavior.**

I learned pageant emcee skills by watching Bob Barker, who, I believe, hosted the Miss USA and Miss Universe Pageants at the time. I could easily tell exactly which contestants he liked and didn't like.

I thought that was a very poor choice on his part. However, it taught me a great deal about what I considered proper and respectful emcee decorum. It taught me how *not* to behave.

Other examples of bad behavior teaching us lessons come all too frequently from professional athletes. I call the bad boys "Testosterone Toddlers," and I am glad when they get ejected from a game for committing heinous personal fouls.

Being a professional in any field unfortunately does <u>not</u> require behaving in a professional manner. It sometimes simply means that a person gets paid for what they do. One can be a professional actor or a professional teacher. One can behave professionally, or one can behave unprofessionally.

Remember tennis pro Serena Williams at the U.S. Open in September 2018? Rather than taking personal responsibility for her own ranting, she charged the umpire with sexual discrimination, saying that men get away with ranting all the time.

Okayyyyy. Even if they do or did, that does not make it right for her or anyone else! Smashing tennis racquets and screaming down an umpire reflects childish, emotional lack of control. (Yes, Testosterone Toddlers can be women, too.) This example became even more sad when Williams' coach admitted that he had indeed been coaching her from the box, the activity that inspired the umpire's calls and Williams' outbursts.

Meanwhile, a 20-year-old Naomi Osaka was not discouraged nor deterred, going on to beat Williams and become the first Japanese to win a Grand Slam. Staying focused must have been quite challenging as she watched an idol and major star melt down.

Williams could have complained formally and let the young champion have her well-earned moment in the spotlight without sullying up the water, so to speak. Ah, yes. Could have. Should have. Didn't.

Life isn't fair. How we look at life and respond to its challenges is, however, a matter of choice.

Remember, Ginger Rogers did everything Fred Astaire did, but she did it backwards and in high heels. Sometimes, no matter who we are, we must work harder and overcome more than others.

## Fairness is rarely dealt out fairly.

So, while we are lightening things up here, please pardon the pun, but how many Discouragers does it take to screw in a lightbulb? What does it matter? It's just going to burn out again anyway.

Discouragers behave negatively. Negative behaviors create negative people. Avoiding negative people is important to our mental health, attitude, and success in life. We can't always do that. So, we need to learn how to manage discouragement and Discouragers.

First, that means recognizing how they drain us physically, mentally, and emotionally. Discouragers can leave us feeling tense or tired, worrying, feeling cynical or irritable. We don't need any of that. That leads to burn out.

## The most important thing to do is to recognize a Discourager as a Discourager.

Don't accept their excuses for any of it. They put others down, believing only they are right. They judge others, and yet struggle to admit their own mistakes. They bully and intimidate. They criticize and lack respect. They are pessimistic.

We all know Discouragers. As we've said, a superb key to survive and thrive their discouragement is to consider the source. We do this compassionately by not judging their position, but by recognizing the impact *we* are permitting their negativity to have on us.

If someone is not lifting us up, they are holding us down. We need not accept their drivel as ours. We can recognize that they may be confused. We can accept that they, just as all of us, have a long way to grow. We can accept that we need not adopt their inconsistencies, self-centered attitudes, or priorities.

Whenever possible, reduce contact with Discouragers. I always support folks who ache because they've had to let certain people go. Sometimes this means blocking or removing social media contacts, such as Facebook Friends. I have friends who even had to block family members from their social media accounts.

It's never easy to block out close friends or family members. However, for your own survival and mental health, sometimes it becomes essential. Family members and friends love us. They should never slam us or try to shame us because we think or feel differently than they do. My heart always aches when people go through this challenge.

I feel so very blessed that my family members have always been totally supportive of each other, even when our opinions stand diametrically opposed. While there are topics we may avoid bringing up when certain family members are with us, we also remain in full support of each other, regardless.

I think that's healthy. Anything less needs work.

We all need to try to block out negative, even when it seems overwhelming. Look for even the slightest positive expression or love that a Discourager exudes. Appreciate them for that.

We've often heard of "selective listening," typically in a comic reflection after a husband says he has "tuned out his wife's voice." But we can apply that thinking in a positive, though purely external way when bombarded by a Discourager's garbage.

We do this by not letting their words or efforts get to our hearts. Don't let them wound us. Don't let them sour our souls.

This is easy to say in words, but we can struggle with it in practice. Sometimes we feel overwrought by it all, overflowing with hopelessness, slammed into the proverbial wall. We can feel we simply cannot take any more.

Start by being patient with yourself. Promise yourself to be true to yourself and your goals. Remind yourself that you are worthy and do not need to buy into a Discourager's rhetoric.

## A fabulous choice is to also surround yourself with Encouragers.

They will give you strength and confidence. We all need that.

If you feel that you are or have been a Discourager yourself, look at some of the things that can eradicate such tendencies. Try focusing on the other person and truly listening to what they are trying to say. Try to imagine feeling the way they do. Try to see a situation from their perspective.

I recall a great lesson in this in a debate club. We were always told the issue to be debated, but we did not know to which side of the issue we would be assigned. We had to prepare to represent both sides of the argument. That builds perspective.

## We don't have to agree with both sides of an issue to have genuine interest in gaining perspective.

We need not become some fictious "Pollyanna Purebred" sort of character. Everything is not perfect. However, we don't need to don rose-colored glasses to think and see positively. We do need to make decisions every day to *not* be naysayers, to break habits of expressing negative views or complaining, to criticize and cast doubt less.

## We do not need to strive to be average.

I've always been told that "average" is the best of the worst and the worst of the best, not a goal for which to strive. My parents encouraged us to strive to be our best, the best that we could be. They never said strive to be average.

We can all do that. Strive to be our very best, whatever that may be. Learn to disregard the negative input from Discouragers.

## Hit flush!

Recognize that Discouragers are projecting *their* fears, negativity, or lack of confidence onto others. Remember, it's *their* pity party. Do not attend.

If we are up for the task, we may even invite them to leave the pity party behind. Whether they accept the fact or not, we can gently and sincerely try to help them realize that their discouragement reflects on *their* attitude, not *ours*.

We must expect to get pushback from a Discourager. They are not prone to openly recognize areas in which they could improve.

However, if you can compassionately state the facts about how they are hurting themselves and others, it is a valuable beginning. Making that position known is also empowering for you.

And who knows? Just maybe, the Discourager will have an epiphany!

**Tip:**
*It's a very funny thing about life;*
*if you refuse to accept anything but the best, you very often get it.*
-- William Somerset Maugham
(1874 -- 1965)
British Playwright & Novelist

Photo Credit: Louis Hansel

Rust Buster #4
# Encouragement versus Motivation

> *But words are things, and a small drop of ink,*
> *Falling like dew, upon a thought, produces*
> *That which makes thousands, perhaps millions, think...*
> -- Lord Byron  (1788 – 1824)
> British Poet & Politician

Both motivation and encouragement play important roles in our journeys. We can give and get motivation and encouragement. While they are often seen as similar, there are some subtle and not-so-subtle differences.

Motivation involves inspiration to try or do something that typically has a reward associated with attainment or victory. Motivation boosts our willingness or enthusiasm about undertaking a task and provides reason to take interest in something or some course of action.

Encouragement persuades us to stay on course toward our goals. Encouragement gives support, improves our confidence, and may even include counseling or assistance toward that goal.

As with encouragement, we can be motivated both internally and externally. As with encouragement, motivation comes in many forms and varies from person to person. Money may motivate one person, but not another. Others may strive for power or a promotion. We can't be motivated by something we already have as much of as we want. If you already have money, cash incentives won't likely motivate you. If you already got the promotion or job you want, there's little to motivate you to want a new job.

We can be motivated when we perceive a void in our lives. We can be motivated to want to fill the void or change something in our situation. We can be motivated to make a change because we want the results the change will bring.

However, once motivated, we likely perform better and succeed faster when we receive encouragement. For example, I may be motivated to lose weight because I want to fit into my clothing better. I will assuredly need encouragement along the way because I love to eat… all the wrong food.

We do certain things to help ensure desired outcomes… or avoid undesired ones. For example, we may set a daily alarm clock, so we get up and get to work on time to not get in trouble with our boss. Fear of failure, be it large or small, can be a powerful driving force. There may also be a fear of change.

## Humans are highly resistant to change.

External rewards are powerful. We need to pay the rent, so our paycheck is motivating. Our motivation in this case comes out of a sense of necessity. We need to survive… eat, find shelter, and such.

Internal motivators can be even more powerful. These can be personal goals or growth challenges we set for ourselves. Sometimes, it might just feel good to do simple things, like opening the door for someone or taking half an hour each day to meditate.

## Internal motivators often reveal our driving forces.

We may simply want to do things that will result in fun, or we may try something because curiosity was our motivation. Or, in addition to the responsibility of supporting our family, we may want to make them feel proud of us. We may feel a powerful need to be perceived by others, even our close friends, as successful.

Again, when we are motivated to do something, there is a reward at the end, be it physical, spiritual, or emotional. Motivation stimulates or influences us to do something. It instills a desire to pursue a goal.

When we are encouraged to do something, there is a strengthening of our resolve or a boosting of our confidence. Encouragement endorses our purpose and builds our hope that we can continue despite challenges and difficulties. It instills courage to persevere.

Many people start a day or begin a task with a get-up-and-go attitude. They may be called self-starters or self-motivated people.

However, most of us need, or at least appreciate, some encouragement along the way. We get tired. When we grow weary, doubts creep into our minds. We may wonder if the effort is worth the eventual outcome. Encouragement builds and boosts our strength and resolve to keep on going and working toward our goal. Encouragement acknowledges our efforts and achievements and assures us that we are on the right and worthy track.

We encourage a friend who has been ill or feeling down by reminding them that they are not alone. We are standing by them. They will get through this.

# Encouragement

We motivate a friend by showing them the light at the end of the tunnel. We are trying to inspire them to take some action, even if it is simply to follow doctor's orders to heal or bounce back from some illness. They may well need regular encouragement along a long path. Pain, disappointment, setbacks, or just a lot of passing time can be demoralizing and make goals feel increasingly elusive.

Friends can be both motivating and encouraging. Close friends, particularly those we most trust, make us work harder, feel stronger, persevere longer. We add to our resolve when we have people we don't want to let down. The Encouragers in our circles of friends acknowledge our little forward steps and remind us that we can make it all the way.


*A little progress each day adds up to big results.*
-- Anonymous


Little quips and longer quotations can be quite motivating or encouraging. Seek and see them everywhere you can, from books and social media postings to posters and T-shirts.

Whether your motivation is physical, such as for financial reward, or a desire for internal growth, or a spiritual desire to help others have better lives, motivation is vital. Even if you have a powerful desire to change the world or even your corner of it, seek out and embrace all the encouragement you can along the way to help stay the course.


**Tip:** While motivation fires up our interest and willingness to run the race, encouragement helps get us across the finish line.

Rust Buster #5
# Deftly Deal with Despair

*Accept the challenges so that you can feel the exhilaration of victory.*
–George S. Patton (1885 – 1945)
United States Army General

We all go through challenges. Some are large. Some are small. As we approach some challenges, we stumble. At other times, we overcome the storms and find those rays of sunshine.

Think about it. What are some of the difficult scenarios that you overcame last week? Last month? Last year? At any point in your life?

During the darkest moments, something gave you strength... hope... faith... confidence... the ability to persist... to hang on... to keep on trying. Something helped you to overcome.

*In the middle of every difficulty lies opportunity.*
- Albert Einstein (1879 – 1955)
German Physicist

In a time of particular political divisiveness, I recall Reverend Linda Johnson offering a prayer asking leaders to make decisions to help the least, the last, and the lost among us. I loved those words, "the least, the last, and the lost among us."

I don't know of anyone who has not felt very much within that group at various times in life. Do you?

That is when we feel discouraged. The days feel dark. We feel unsure of a path to follow to find the sun again. If we have faith, we may well find great encouragement in the words spoken by a pastor or in the Bible.

Once a year, another favorite pastor, Mark Williams at the United Church of Marco Island, tells a favorite story about a child who is befriended by the local telephone operator, which helps them both through various challenges.

The theme is one of hope, reminding us that even in times of great loss, we need to have faith. There are other worlds in which to sing. In some of life's darkest moments, that is something important to remember.

The story, "Information Please," was written by Paul Villiard. It is one of those delightfully engaging tales often shared through emails.

However, it was written long before there was an Internet and was originally published in 1966 by Reader's Digest. I can never read nor hear that story without a few tears sliding down my cheek.

**Trade in our cynical hopelessness
for cynical hopefulness.
If we must be cynical,
choose hopeful over hopeless.**

We do not have to lose hope. We need not flounder in despair and discouragement.

Yet, we are mere humans. We often need help finding the right direction. Believe it or not, a great deal of information and help can be found in an active, loving, happy congregation. No matter what your faith may be, finding a place that fills your heart and soul with love and hope and encouragement will work wonders in times of despair.

Many verses in the Bible are great to read and re-read, especially in times when we need to deal with despair. Consider just a few from the book of Proverbs.

*A gentle answer turns away wrath, but a harsh word stirs up anger.*
-- Proverbs 15:1

*Blessed is the one who finds wisdom and the one who gets understanding, for the gain is better than gain from silver and the profit is better than gold.*
-- Proverbs 3:13-14

*The fear of the Lord is the beginning of knowledge, but fools despise wisdom and instruction.*
-- Proverbs 1:7

*A man who is kind benefits himself, but a cruel man hurts himself.*
-- Proverbs 11:17

*A heart at peace gives life to the body, but envy rots the bones.*
-- Proverbs 14:30

*A cheerful heart is good medicine,*
*but a crushed spirit dries up the bones.*
-- Proverbs 17:22

*As iron sharpens iron, so one person sharpens another.*
-- Proverbs 27:17

That last verse reflects another great skill to help us deal deftly with despair. That skill is choosing the people around us.

Some people tend to support us, while others tend to tear people down. We want to find and surround ourselves with the positive people.

That may sound obvious, but we sometimes forget that people are somewhat like the buttons on an elevator. They can either take us up, or they can take us down. We want Encouragers around us, especially in times of despair, when we most need lifting.

*It is when we are most lost*
*that we sometimes find our truest friends.*
– Walt Disney's
"Snow White and the Seven Dwarfs"

A lesson I learned from my father applies here. He never left words unspoken, which I believe is good advice. We never know what twists and turns life will bring. How wonderful would it be if we could all share encouraging words with others, every time we think of them, without delay?

My brother and sister-in-law were with Mom on the last day of Dad's life. They could see he was failing fast and advised me to rush there if I hoped to see him before he died. In just a few hours, he was gone. As I mentioned in the Dedication at the beginning of this book, that was October 6, 2018.

I was not able to make it in time, and yet that was somehow alright. I knew that no words between us had gone unspoken. That was Dad's way.

So, we mourned. We also celebrated the wonderful man that my father truly was.

## Great memories really can help overwhelm grief.

And despair. When times seem the toughest, I try not to wring my hands. I try not to fret over what might have been. I try not to get caught up in the "could have, would have, should have" trap.

Instead, I try to recall the many wonderful things about this place we call Life. I do not permit myself to believe that everything is bleak.

> *It always seems impossible until it is done.*
> - Nelson Mandela (1918-2013)
> President of South Africa 1994-1999

Encouragement can also come from some surprising directions. While it can be unexpected, encouragement is always welcome.

Have you ever seriously broken a leg or hip? Or been bedridden by surgery or an illness that just doesn't seem to want to go away? Or felt so much pain that despair seemed to be the only possible emotion?

I understand. Recently, I was overdoing while performing some tasks, and I completely threw out my lower back. Nothing seemed to help. Ice packs. Hot shower. Heating pad. Stretching. Back exercises. Lying down. Massage. Nothing.

When I tried to get out of bed in the morning, it took a full half hour. Pain pierced straight through me with every attempt to move. Ever so gradually I would get to my feet, only to have each tiny step send another lightning bolt of agony up my back.

Sitting in a straight back chair or lying in bed seemed comfortable. However, trying to then move or stand up changed everything. And not for the better.

As this went on day after day, I started wondering if it might be my new "normal." Not an exciting thought, I know.

**In pain and sickness,
it takes a lot of strength and courage
to envision life without pain or sickness.**

We become more susceptible to despair in such conditions. That is only natural. Learning to thwart despair can be just as natural. A good sense of humor helps, as does not taking ourselves too seriously.

Regardless of what is going on in our lives, we have the strength and power to alter our perspective. We can think of lighter, more pleasant times. We can ponder things we would like to do when the bleak situation abates. We can busy ourselves with whatever activities and events are possible. We can stop focusing on the negative.

We are allowed to scream. We're allowed to cry. But we must not give up.

This too shall pass. This is only temporary.

**Tip:** Think of the words of American poet and civil rights activist, Maya Angelou, who lived from 1928 till 2014. As commencement speaker at my college graduation, her message was clear on despair. She said, "We may encounter defeats, but we must not be defeated."

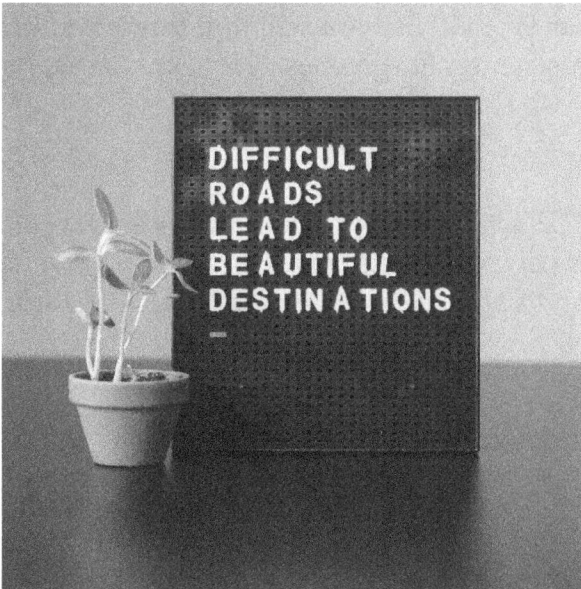

Rust Buster #6
## Super Six Skill Set

*Life is 10% what happens to you and 90% how you react to it.*
-- Charles R. Swindoll  (1934 - )
American Pastor, Author & Educator

There are a great many skills that help us as people and as Encouragers.  Here we will look at six that can truly and rapidly evolve our personal mindsets.

These can help us become successful in both our personal and professional lives.  Better yet?  There is no cost to gaining these skills.  We pay nothing.  We give up nothing.  We each gain everything, including lots of credits toward earning our MBE as a Morale Booster Extraordinaire.

In the Super Six Skill Set you will find important basics.  They include Persistence, Forgiveness, Honesty, Trust, Patience, and Generosity.

*Character cannot be developed in ease and quiet.*
*Only through experience of trial and suffering can the soul be*
*strengthened, ambition inspired, and success achieved.*
-- Helen Keller (1880 – 1968)
American Author, Activist & Lecturer

Being a character may be simple, but no one says being of good character is easy.  However, we've likely all heard it said on more than one occasion that we rarely, if ever, meet a strong person with a weak past.

We are weak or strong, one or the other. We might as well build some super skills that also build strong character.

## Persistence

> *Never, never, never give up.*
> -- Winston Churchill (1874 – 1965)
> British Statesman & Prime Minister

Some people seem to have an easy time with Life. We all know them. They get A's in school, seemingly without studying. They excel in sports, seeming like superior, natural athletes. They get promotions at work, seeming to turn everything they touch to gold.

What we don't see is how hard they may have worked for the achievement. Most of us learn gradually. We learn by observing. We learn by doing. We learn by trying. We learn by failing. Repeatedly.

## Remember, it's getting up, not falling down that matters.

Some of Life's lessons are even more valuable when our achievements take more time and effort. We are learning to not give up. We are learning to repeat, again and again, the exercises and actions that will bring success.

In business, we learn we must often try, try, and try again to make the deal work. In sports, we learn we must repeat again, and again, and again the moves that will prove successful on offense or defense.

In the military, we learn that repetition turns behaviors and skills into automatic responses. In all facets of life, we can rarely do something once and expect it to stay done.

We must learn to try and try again. We humans do not always do everything exactly right. However, when we persist, we turn good actions into habits. Positive choices made repeatedly become seemingly automatic.

## Sometimes the brightest lights come out of the darkest corners.

We may feel down-trodden or hopeless, exhausted or helpless. These are the times we must focus on the need to persist. We must pick ourselves up and try again.

I've heard musicians laugh when media dubbed them as an overnight success. The artists know that they've often spent years, even decades, honing their skills. Persisting. Trying again and again and again, even when it appeared hopeless.

Suddenly, they had a big gig. They appear to have emerged out of nowhere. An overnight success! Nope. Perhaps a 20-year success. They came out of the land of persistence.

*Press on. Nothing can take the place of persistence. Talent will not; nothing is more common than unsuccessful men with talent. Genius will not; unrewarded genius is almost a proverb. Education will not; the world is full of educated derelicts. Perseverance and determination alone are omnipotent.*
-- Calvin Coolidge (1872 – 1933)
30th President of the United States

Persistency is a valuable tool to place prominently in your success skill set, both personally and professionally. So, say a little prayer. Tie a little knot. Hang in there!

*Our greatest weakness lies in giving up. The most certain way to succeed is always to try just one more time.*
-- Thomas A. Edison  (1847 -1931)
American Inventor & Businessman

## Forgiveness

Often, when we least expect it, anger gets in our way. It jumps right up and bites us. It may snap. It may rage out of control. Anger is nasty.

We humans tend to harbor our feelings, both positive and negative, anchoring them securely within our hearts. This may protect us from getting hurt, or so we believe. But it does not prevent us from hurting others. This not only limits the love we can share, but it restricts our total quality of life.

**We remember the hurt, the injustice, and the trauma, but we can forgive the sinner.**

Learning to genuinely forgive is key. We need not forget.

Never mind the old saying, "Forgive and forget." When we learn to genuinely forgive, we get to still remember and yet not succumb to the urge to throw some hurtful reminder of a misdeed in the face of a loved one.

Forgiving means we accept someone's sincere apology. We understand we are mere humans, and thus, highly imperfect.

We appreciate someone's true conviction to not repeat hurtful behavior. We have let go of all anger and resentment for the harm they have caused us or other loved ones.

Though never easy, forgiving someone becomes even more challenging when the offender has not made a sincere apology. Some people lack that ability in their skill sets, even when they feel absolute remorse for their deeds or words that caused pain and harm.

We can still forgive them, whether or not we or others may feel they are deserving. When we do forgive, especially under the most difficult circumstances, we grow and evolve as people.

Even more challenging? Self-forgiveness. It is hard to apologize to ourselves. We tend to simply beat ourselves up over harsh words we spoke out of emotion. We sometimes try to rationalize or justify our misdeeds to feel more validated or worthy.

We need to let it go. Let our hearts feel absolved. Let our souls commit to doing better. In the meantime, as we progress along our personal paths, we fare far better if we are not allowing feelings of unworthiness or self-loathing to hold us back.

*The courage to be is the courage to accept oneself,*
*in spite of being unacceptable.*
-- Paul Tillich  (1886 – 1965)
German-American Philosopher

All of us have things we wish we could un-do. The bell cannot be un-rung.

However, self-loathing can and must be forgiven if we are to progress. And we do deserve to progress.

This also sets a powerful example for those we may mentor. To be worthy mentors, we need not be perfect, thank God! We merely need to be trying to do our best to be good people.

Let It Go!


## Honesty

Challenging is often the best way to describe being honest with ourselves. We all tend to lie to ourselves about various aspects of life.


## Adding more bull to bull yields bigger bull.


Perhaps we tell ourselves that we ate healthy on a day when we've conveniently forgotten the cake, cookies, or candy we munched between meals. Or the three beers we downed after work with friends that evening.

Maybe we tell ourselves that we are trying as hard as we can to succeed in our work. However, perhaps we are doing well what everyone else is doing. We are not going above and beyond the norm. We are not actually giving it our all.

This is all okay. We all goof up. We can turn the page and start fresh the next day.

*A person who never made a mistake never tried anything new.*
– Albert Einstein (1879 – 1955)
German Physicist

We can lie to ourselves in big and little ways. And we can do it so often that we no longer notice our own dishonesty. We become like our own little politicians if we keep repeating a lie frequently and vehemently enough that even we start to believe it. Sorry, but it's still not true.

That said, I'm a fan of the "fake it till you make it" line of thinking, but only when we don't take it literally. I do not suggest buying a new sports car every year when you can't afford it. I am referring to practicing the ability to claim the positive, even when we may be living in very negative circumstances.

Positive self-talk should be meant to recognize our efforts and lift our spirits to try again and to try harder. We are not lying to ourselves. We are encouraging ourselves.

This is paralleled by our positive reinforcement of a friend's efforts. We are not lying when we applaud what someone has done or tried to do, even when they did not achieve their highest goal.

We are not lying to a child when we encourage them by saying, "You can do it," as they struggle to learn to ride a bicycle, falling off several times.

We are claiming the positive, reinforcing our and their belief in an ability, and recognizing their positive efforts.

**Honesty begins with each of us.**
**We need to be honest with ourselves**
**before we can truly be honest with others.**

No one is impressed by somebody living a lie. That is simply sad. When honesty with someone is painful, we must be strong enough to be the most gentle. Get them alone. Be sure they know you care deeply about them and their happiness. Take caution to not ever appear judgmental.

Honesty leaves everyone with a clear conscience and a loving heart.

## Trust

*As soon as you trust yourself, you will know how to live.*
-- Johann Wolfgang von Goethe
(1749-1832)
German Writer & Statesman

Trust can be a tricky skill. People break our trust far too often, sometimes unintentionally. We learn to distrust after great repetition of broken trust, not some isolated incident. We learn to trust in the very same way.

Look at people you may know who have earned a trustworthy reputation. They built that foundation. They proved trustworthiness with multiple people, in various capacities, over many years. We have confidence they will not let us down.

# Encouragement

When someone has a well-earned reputation for being untrustworthy, we can still trust them. We can trust they will behave in a certain manner, though not one we may seek nor prefer. We have confidence they will likely let us down.

When meeting someone new, I like to give them the benefit of the doubt. A clean slate. That means learning to not transfer my past fears and learned distrust to this new scenario.

This does not mean throwing all caution to the wind. We need not be foolish. I remember President Ronald Reagan often repeating the phrase, "Trust, but verify."

Of course, he was referring to the tenuous relationship the USA had with the Soviet Union as he worked to end the Cold War between our nations. Reagan was willing to accept their word, but he also exercised caution. He wanted to verify and validate information. He did not offer blind trust.

We rarely need to be so extreme in our personal relationships. That said, verifying is quite easy now with the Internet and social media. I admit, that I do proceed with more caution when someone tends not to be an open-book sort of person.

While it is difficult and quite often more painful, I prefer to trust someone openly from the start. It's on them if they prove to be unworthy of my trust. Recall the saying, "Fool me once, shame on you. Fool me twice, shame on me." That says trust, but do not expect some untrustworthy cat to change his spots after scratching you once.

However, it's ultimately more fulfilling to trust someone upfront, especially when people turn out to be well-worthy.

## Patience

*Someone has defined genius as intensity of purpose: the ability to do, the patience to wait… Put these together and you have genius, and you have achievement.*
-- Leo Joseph Muir (1880 – 1967)
American Educator & Author

Microwave mentality makes patience a challenging skill. So, we can bake a potato in 5 minutes now, rather than sixty. Still, we are anxious to push the "stop" button on the microwave a few seconds early. We hate to wait.

Time is a very precious commodity. Regardless, situations often include circumstances that are beyond our control.

## We do best when we do not allow challenges to negatively affect our attitude.

When three lanes of traffic on the highway come to a full stop, we are not the only people whose lives are affected. Dozens or hundreds of other people have just had their schedules unwittingly altered, as well.

If a serious accident is the cause of the back-up, those people's lives have been altered far more dramatically than ours. If it's merely construction or a breakdown causing the delay, so be it.

## Squawking and barking help nothing and no one.

Try to allow extra time when traveling, to have a better chance of avoiding frustration. Meanwhile, use a hands-free telephone device to make good use of the extended windshield time. Or find good music on the radio and sing along. Or, if there are others in the car, enjoy some conversation.

This is just a look at patience on the road. Patience applies to every other scenario as well.

Being patient daily shows that we have an awareness of and appreciation for people around us. Patience may not always come easily. Patience may take practice, especially to apply it to those closest to us.

We can learn to ask for help patiently, rather than snapping. We can use a pleasant tone, rather than exuding a nasty or demanding slant. We can calmly involve others in schedule planning, rather than forcing our will on someone. We can sincerely ask how someone is feeling or doing, and then truly listen to their answers, rather than taking others for granted as we zoom through our lives.

Practicing negative emotion self-restraint and tolerance may not be the norms today, but if we try to do a better job with patience, the world will be a better place.

## Generosity

*I learned long ago that those who are happiest*
*are those who do the most for others.*
-- Booker T. Washington  (1856 – 1915)
American Educator
Presidential Advisor

We can be generous or stingy in many ways. Consider money, time, and kindness. Being generous or not is a personal choice. Our time on Earth is a short run, even if we live for a full Century. I contend that we live far happier lives when we are generous in as many ways as possible.

When I have money, I have shared it. When I have time, I have shared it. Those are two areas where we may have more or less available, both for ourselves, as well as to offer others.

Yes, we all have the same 24-hours per day, but we also each have different circumstances that require varying amounts of our time. Demands from work, health, and family are just a few factors to consider.

Regardless of time or money resources, kindness is an area in which we can and should all be generous. It costs no money to be kind. It takes no extra time to be kind.

Someone holds open a door for you. Say, "Thank you." If someone is approaching a door, open and hold it open for them. Those are easy scenarios that show common decency and respect.

**I am calling for uncommon decency.**
**Respect that comes from awareness.**

Have you ever been in a vehicle and observed another driver behaving as if they are the only car on the road? This happens in many ways. For example, you may have been sitting at an intersection waiting for traffic to pass. Although you are clearly waiting, a driver may fail to signal that they are going to turn, so you need not have waited.

Or you may be on a highway, where two lanes are merging into one, and most people behave respectfully, alternating cars from each lane. Then, along comes that driver who is, obviously, too important to merge into one lane by awaiting his turn with everyone else. Instead, he zooms up to the front of the line and cuts in.

Kindness is a lot like respect. These drivers are showing their disregard for other people. We all have good and bad days. Showing respect and showing kindness are worthy habits to develop. We can be kind all day, every day, regardless of our time or financial restraints.

## It requires neither time nor money to be kind.

It's easy to be kind. Smile and say, "Good day" to people. Treat them as we would all like to be treated. Share a few pleasant or appreciative or supportive words with someone. With kindness, we can each become the most generous people in the world.

Be proud if kindness can be your legacy.

**Tip:**
*It is time for us all to stand and cheer for the doer, the achiever – the one who recognizes the challenges and does something about it.*
-- Vince Lombardi  (1913 – 1970)
American NFL Coach

Rust Buster #7
## Create Habits to Live By

*Quality if not an act; it is a habit.*
-- Aristotle  (384 – 322 B.C.)
Greek Philosopher

Good habits are not created easily.  They take time and a great deal of discipline and persistence.  As with any skill, we are not going to master creating good habits in one day.  That would be like thinking we could master the rest of our lives in just one day.  Riiight!

We need to do just one good thing toward creating that habit.  Then we need to do it again the next day.  And every day.  No one starts out as an expert.  Don't sweat it.

*Start where you are.  Use what you have.  Do what you can.*
-- Arthur Ashe  (1943 – 1993)
American Professional Tennis Player

Arthur Ashe walked the walk.  He worked hard at his craft daily.  He developed great habits that eventually brought him great success, including being the first black tennis player selected to the United States Davis Cup Team.  Ashe is also the only black man to win the singles title at Wimbledon, the U.S. Open, and the Australian Open.

We may not ever aspire toward such greatness, but we can aspire to develop good habits to bring ourselves happier, healthier daily lives.  We can't just talk the talk.

We must make it real. Making it real starts with our attitude.

I believe a great attitude is developed just as any good habit. I know that I had a wretchedly poor attitude as a pre-teen. It took years of constant work to shift gears and see the world differently. I needed to develop an attitude of gratitude. Thankfully, I did.

That is the perfect starting point, and I still recommend it for all of us. This means slightly different things to each of us.

However, at the core are some basics. I found it helpful to learn to see and appreciate all facets of my life. When cranky people seem all around us, this can be challenging. But it's worthwhile. Our hearts are healed, and our attitudes improved each time we express thankfulness for the big and little things around us.

As my Mom used to tell me, "You can make your bed with a smile, or you can make your bed with a frown. But you are going to make your bed."

She was right about lots of things. She gave me the power to choose what kind of attitude I would have. I could choose to be grumpy or happy. Hmmm.

## Which way would make Life more enjoyable?

I figured it out. And I have applied her lesson countless times since. Start with creating or strengthening a good attitude habit, and each day will become genuinely brighter. Life will be more promising. We will be more encouraging.

Another great habit to live by is to become a conversation starter. No matter what someone may be going through, it can be most helpful to be offered a safe, non-threatening environment in which to talk it out.

Even if we think we know absolutely nothing about the topic at hand, we can still ask someone a question. We can listen. We can learn. We could even ask a person how they might explain or introduce the topic to someone who knew nothing about it. We can ask them to tell us more.

We are giving them credibility. We are validating their opinion or information as worthy. Everyone needs that.

Developing an uplifting habit is also great. Don't we all prefer to be around people who lift us up, rather than people who stress us out or bring us down?

I find it helps to smile. That makes me feel better, and it also seems to automatically make someone else smile, too. Sometimes it helped me when I wrote down something every day that made me happy or made me smile or even laugh.

When I hear people expressing angst because some friend just caused them tremendous heartache and grief, it would be easy (and often flippant) to tell them to simply ignore the negative friend or consider the source. Of course, unless done compassionately, that is a "put down" of their friend. That is not my intention.

Instead, I learned to try to express a sort of acceptance of the good and bad in the world. However, along with that I try to offer a reminder that when someone is determined to be utterly sour, we need not drink their lemonade.

That's somewhat like refusing to join someone's pity party. Again, I stress the need to actively protect ourselves from negative onslaughts. A great habit to create is to stay calm when all about seem to be losing their minds.

Another wonderful habit is to try to genuinely see someone else's vision, opinion, or perspective, regardless of how different it may be from our own thoughts. This is not to say that we must change our thinking. I merely think it's healthy when we can learn to support someone else's position by providing them with feedback that both bolsters their confidence and reflects our open-minded attitude.

It hurts no one when we offer up kind words to let someone know they've done a good job. In fact, it helps.

## Be one of a kind and be one with human kind.

To be positive with other people, we need to start by being positive with ourselves. It's easy to get down on ourselves. But if we are in a dark place, how can we expect to shine a light on anyone or anything else?

Look for small efforts. Try not to expect great or grandiose things from ourselves or others. And yet, recognize even the smallest effort that someone has made. It's far too common to get caught up finding fault and missing what someone has completed.

For example, if someone worked all afternoon weeding extensive flowerbeds, they may have run out of steam before getting through them all. I may see a section that they did not get done and overlook all the work they accomplished.

An encouraging recognition comment might be, "Wow! Look how awesome the gardens are where you worked. Beautiful!" A demoralizing choice might be to say something like, "Well, if you started earlier in the day you might have gotten it *all* done." All such a comment succeeds in doing is making the person believe they can never please me.

I'll stress it again. We don't realize sometimes just how powerful our words are. If we only see the big picture, we might miss the little steps along the way.

A far better habit is finding positive things to think and say daily. This also helps us reject negative thoughts and words. They often come when we least need them, especially from folks who seem to have a bad case of "Stinking Thinking." We need to build up our defenses.

I saw a funny T-shirt saying. "Whether you see the glass as half empty or half full, I need more wine." That's quippy and cute, but we feel much better about ourselves, our lives, and everyone around us when we see the glass as half full.

That reflects positive thinking. That means we are less apt to be dragging ourselves down, or anyone else. Folks who see the glass as half empty, tend to be fault-finders, complainers, nasty perfectionists. We are happier and healthier when we don't have days like that, never mind have lives like that.

No one expects anyone to be perky and positive 100% of the time. There are natural ups and downs in Life. However, creating a habit of seeking the bright side of a situation is never negative. It always helps when we learn to not see the worst in people first. Try to see the best in someone, even when it is frustratingly difficult to see.

The same goes for learning to "bite our tongue" when we feel upset or tired or stressed. We do not gain anything positive when we lash out verbally. We need to build a few verbal filters that help us not sound nasty or hateful. We don't want to be shallow people. We don't want to get involved in gossip and rumors. If we stumble, apologize. And mean it.

A friend of ours, Bill Andrews, shared a philosophy that has helped him work with challenging people. He says to have no expectations, and you'll not feel let down by people. We dubbed that the Andrews Principle. While it sounded a bit funny at first, it works. It's only when we expect someone to do or say specific things that they can let us down by not living up to expectations we had placed on them.

Another great habit to create is tolerance. Yes, it can become a habit. When ideas fly in our faces that are contradictory to what we believe is right, we tend to react. Tolerance teaches us to calmly examine what is happening, open our minds and perspective, and allow and encourage differing beliefs.

## When we fail to be tolerant of others, we fail.

Frank Mallicoat, a friend and former television broadcasting colleague of mine, works as an anchor at a station serving the San Francisco, California market. Each day he uses social media to post questions for the viewers. On August 30, 2018, Frank's "Question of the Day" noted that the corporate arm of the "In & Out Burger" chain had donated $25-thousand to the California Republican Party. He asked if people would still get burgers there, or if politics would keep them away?

Responses flew fast and furiously. I was rather pleased that most felt we should keep politics out of our daily lives, expressing tolerance and respect. Naturally, others vehemently said they were furious and DONE supporting the business.

## My philosophy of Boomerang Bullying comes to mind.

When detractors start railing against a company for their political leaning, it inspires many of us to defend whoever is being bullied. A natural human response is to protect someone or something being bullied.

Personally, I do not recall ever having been to an "In & Out Burger" restaurant. That said, like most of us, if bullies rally against them (or anyone else) for their political views, and I am drawn to support them... BIG time.

I'm not alone. Time and time again we've seen it... Boomerang Bullying. The intentionally targeted victim of the negative outcry ends up enjoying more success, often dramatically so.

## We folks in Middle America tend to be unimpressed with bullies or political correctness.

We only all win when we choose to be positive. Screaming or fighting against someone just because they hold different political beliefs draws people and support to *their* side.

I think the Boomerang Bullying reasoning is clear. Bullies come across as narrow-minded and intolerant. While most of us are drawn to people who are tolerant, we are put off by those expressing hatred and intolerance. We support victims.

Tolerance is a habit we can all live by. None of us is 100% right, nor 100% wrong.

**Whether we are happy or sad, grateful or resentful, positive or negative, we are equally precious and deserving.**

Believe it or not, being positive takes courage. Kindness takes courage. Gentleness takes courage. Courage is a great habit to develop because moving through Life peacefully and happily seems to require more and more of it.

We live in a world where it too often seems that "might makes right." People who wield power control our destinies. Folks who scream the loudest get heard, and those who spew the most negative, most repeatedly, get falsely perceived as telling the truth.

Overcoming the discouragement and despair inspired by such drivel requires the habit of courageous kindness. Only kind people are truly tolerant. Only gentle people are truly strong.

Volunteering for and working with Easter Seals, I met some of the most courageous people I know. Many have no luxury of taking good health or a pain-free body for granted. Yet, they smile. They make a habit of finding things to smile about daily. They make kindness to people around them a habit.

Their examples teach us to develop another great habit. Perspective.

When we think we've had a tough day, we likely have. Perhaps we worked on our feet too long. Perhaps the boss was cranky and made everyone's day miserable. Perhaps we dealt with far too many deadlines or negative, demanding people.

For perspective we need only consider the children without legs or use of their legs. The families who lost everything due to fires. The multitudes sold into slavery. Perhaps *our* day wasn't so tough after all.

It takes perspective to recognize that senseless misery in the world can be viewed as purposeful when we let it positively adjust our perspective.

That certainly doesn't ease someone's suffering. However, it provides a positive outcome from something negative.

## Without stormy days, we forget to value sunny skies.

I'll ask again. Can you imagine how wonderful life could be with Encouragers surrounding us? Encouragers running businesses. Encouragers teaching children. Encouragers representing us in Washington, D.C.

Encouragers like cooperation. They value us in the way they want to be valued. So, there's another great habit to live by... Cooperation.

As you can see there are a great many wonderful habits we can create. All these we've mentioned and many more.

We may never get them all wrapped into our daily good habit bundle, but we are better people and better Encouragers with each one we do adapt as our own.

**Tip:** An Encourager makes habits out of envisioning success for themselves and others and teaching us to do the same.

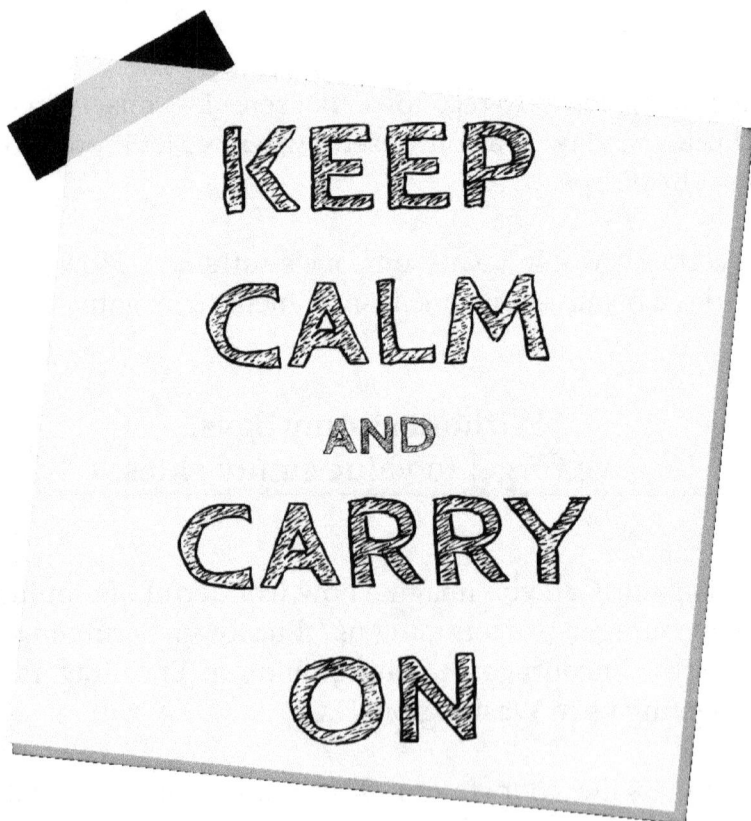

Rust Buster #8
## The Importance of Encouragement

Encouragement energizes us. It empowers us. It makes us accountable to the Encouragers. It bolsters our resolve. It endorses our plans and commitments. It urges us to push forward, regardless of the challenges.

*A word of encouragement during a failure*
*is worth more than an hour of praise after success.*
-- Unknown

The words we speak to someone are more impactful than most of us realize. I recall being shocked the first time a couple of ladies shared with me some words they remembered me offering up as advice decades earlier.

**We tend to wrongfully think that**
**no one would remember our words**
**even minutes later, never mind years.**

So, it's even more important to speak from a position of encouragement. People *do* remember. And negative words haunt us. We are utterly vulnerable to criticism.

Think back. We all have some bleak memories. Perhaps 10 people said how wonderful you looked on a given day. Then one person asked if you were feeling okay, as though they thought you might be coming down with the flu or something. We run off to gaze into our eyes in a mirror. Are we getting sick?

## One negative statement tends to negate an abundance of positive comments.

With all the discouragement around us, the need for encouragement is extremely urgent, not just important. We hear fears and concerns every day. Doomsday talk about the economy, our country, or even the world.

Encouragement empowers us to respond to chaos with logic, sanity, and calmness. We could all use more of that from time to time.

*When one door closes another door opens,*
*but we so often look so long and so regretfully upon the closed door,*
*that we do not see the ones which open for us.*
-- Alexander Graham Bell  (1847 – 1922)
Scottish Scientist and Inventor

I recall hearing how we can divide people into three groups. Those who make things happen, those who watch things happen, and those who wonder what happened. While some people are content to let others take the lead and be "the watchers," none of us wants to land in that third group. No one wants to feel utterly powerless or clueless.

Some people seem naturally comfortable in the driver's seat, making things happen. But they still need encouragement. That gives us confidence in our capabilities. Encouragers instill in us the belief that we can accomplish what we need or want to accomplish.

# The Importance of Encouragement

We all have experienced times when we simply needed someone to say, "You can do this." "You *will* get through this." "You are doing a good job. Stay the course."

Encouragers boost us to take specific steps to overcome obstacles. They make us accountable for our choices. We don't want to let them down. They may be professional associates, friends, neighbors, or family.

*The reason that I am here at all is because of the relationship with my family and their encouragement of me to be a musician and to work hard. As long as I stay there in that space, I can do anything.*
-- Lady Gaga  (1986 - )
American Singer & Actress

We don't all recognize Encouragers. Sometimes we may feel too low to embrace help or even grasp an outreached hand. We may not see the Encourager that compels us to not give up, but they are there trying to help us.

That tends to happen as adults. We have learned to distrust... both other people and ourselves. Again, we have unlearned confidence.

Encouragers help bring us back! They boost our confidence that we are on the right track. They inspire us to carry forward.

*A responsive audience is the best encouragement an actor can have.*
-- Al Jolson  (1886 – 1950)
Russian-born, American Singer & Actor

# Encouragement

Having logged a lot of hours on the theatre stage myself, I understand what Al Jolson meant by that statement. When an audience responds, the actors on stage are encouraged.

Actors may be trying to make them laugh, sit so still you could hear a pin drop, cheer for the hero, or even feel emotion so genuinely that they shed a tear. Actors love drawing an audience into the heart of a story. As drama builds or comedy bubbles, actors are bolstered mightily by the audience's encouragement, delivered assuredly by their responses.

So, imagine the challenge when actors shift to television or film. No live audience. No immediate response. That's like working in a bubble. As they say, a complete paradigm shift is required.

In our daily lives, we typically do not have such isolation. We are not living or working in bubbles, without access to the reactions and responses of others.

Nor are we apt to be living in such isolation that we cannot choose to encourage others. It's important to be both open to encouragement and to offer up sincere encouragement to other people.

We humans have the option to choose or not choose positive thoughts, like hope and optimism. That sounds basic and easy enough. It's not.

We often need encouragement. I say the word "often" with all deliberateness. We don't merely *sometimes* need to feel encouraged. We frequently and repeatedly need it. So, let me repeat myself. We frequently and repeatedly need encouragement.

# The Importance of Encouragement

Each one of us has experienced times when we felt Life or circumstances had overwhelmed us. Without encouragement, we can sink... or at least not swim well. We flounder.

*Optimism is the faith that leads to achievement.*
*Nothing can be done without hope and confidence.*
-- Helen Keller  (1880 – 1968)
American Author, Activist & Lecturer

If we want the most success in our personal and business lives, we must learn to recognize the value of encouragement. The value is almost immeasurable.

**Encouragement makes us believe we can move forward, but it also gives us the power to help others move forward.**

I love the old aphorism that "A rising tide lifts all the boats." When a leader knows to encourage a team, the entire team becomes stronger and far more apt to become successful.

This is true whether we are talking about a team in sports, at work, or in our families. Encouragement to believe in our abilities goes a very long way in helping people achieve goals in all aspects of life.

*What could we accomplish if we knew we could not fail?*
-- Eleanor Roosevelt  (1884 – 1962)
United States First Lady
American Diplomat and Activist

When we encourage, we also help turn other people into Encouragers. When we help someone else grow, everyone scores a true win-win.

**Even when we won't likely learn
whether or not our encouragement
was important to a person,
we shouldn't withhold it.**

Just imagine if down the road someone succeeds because they often recalled encouraging words you had shared. Words that kept them going in times of darkness. Words that gave them confidence to try again. Words that bolstered their belief in their abilities. Words that helped them not give up.

## We hold amazing power in our words.

We can build up someone's confidence or we can tear them down. Power is power, whether we use it for selflessness or selfishness. We can use powerful words to encourage a large group, a small team, or an individual.

A friend on Facebook sent a message with a video of a guy in a truck talking into his dashboard camera. His message was simple. "You are awesome."

The man said it over and over again. He emphasized it was true whether we knew it or not. He called us to action… to share that message with others, because it is so sorely needed in this world.

How very lovely, I thought. I believe I come across as a pretty positive person. Yet, a friend knew that I just might need to hear now and then that I have value. That friend showed his serious Encourager side! (Thank you, Kent Carlson!)

None of us has had a perfect life. Yet, we truly will feel better when we do something to make someone else feel better. Discouragement pounds us down all our lives.

We start out as very free-thinking and expressive individuals. We are then "taught" to feel and behave differently.

We were all told to be quiet when we talked too much as children. Many of us stopped vocally sharing our thoughts and feelings as freely.

We may have dealt with school bus or playground bullies. They set us up to be squelched by other bullies throughout school, work, family, or community endeavors.

We may have become the stereotypical "shrinking violets," as a survival skill. We unlearn that we were designed to blossom fully.

We may have had friends or family members who knowingly or unwittingly taught us to "get along," to not try to reach for lofty goals, to accept that success is meant for others, not us.

We may have had bosses or work associates who lauded power and control over us and never let us forget it. We were nothing. We were replaceable.

**Are we merely taking up space? Hogwash!**

Remember, we need to not delay in sharing our encouraging words for people. If we wait to offer encouraging words, we may lose the opportunity. How many times have we heard of someone's dismay because they wanted to say something to someone, but then the person passed away, without ever hearing the sentiments?

Don't wait for a holiday or birthday or special event to share encouraging words. If you believe it, share it.

## Encouragement from others turns us into Encouragers!

Life can be a very lonely place. When we see someone who has done something worthy of our encouragement, we should tell them. Each time we do that, we are making a positive difference in someone's life, and we are personally growing as Encouragers.

**Tip:** Never let words of encouragement go unsaid.

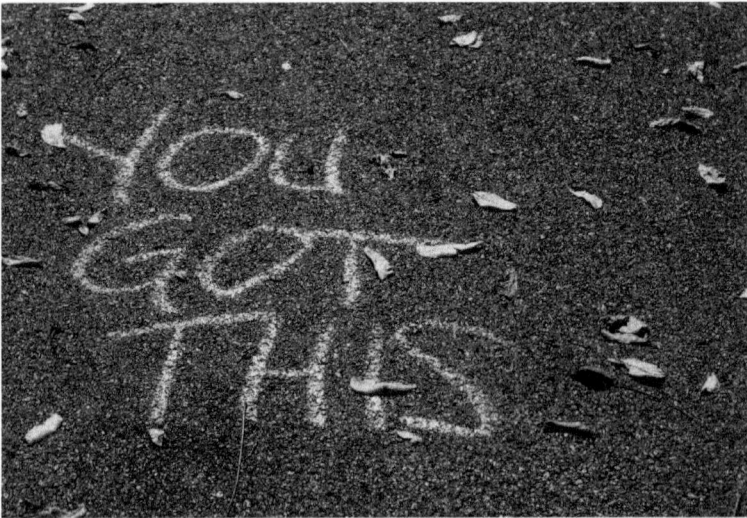

Rust Buster #9
## **Speak and Laugh Freely**

Most of us have known people who seem to flourish with such self-comfort that they communicate easily, without fear or restraint. When they smile or laugh, they light up the room! We may marvel at their self-confidence and relaxed sense of self, which appear unfazed by even a large crowd.

Believe it or not, each of us was born with that same relaxed freedom. As babies, children, and young adults, our freedom of expression gets tamped down by Life, circumstances, and even well-intended adults in our lives.

Babies will giggle and coo without concern. Little children will gush on about whatever topic is foremost in their minds. Young adults bustle with enthusiasm about some goal they have set for themselves.

Sometimes these expressions are supported and encouraged. Then they flourish and grow. Other times, these expressions are squelched and pooh-poohed. Then they falter and whither.

A person may have spent a great deal of time, energy, and thought developing a plan, only to have it thoughtlessly dashed by someone else. This is particularly challenging when that detracting someone is a person in whom we hold a lot of stock.

When we deeply respect someone, we want to make them proud of us. At the very least, we want them to think well of us. We very much need their endorsement of our efforts, dreams, and goals.

# Encouragement

Every time someone tells a child to quiet down, use their "indoor voice," or stop talking, they may be signaling that the child is not worthy. They can deliberately or inadvertently end up devaluing that child by communicating to them that no one wants to hear them.

This is not to say that there are not a great many circumstances in which unrestricted talk or laughter would be unacceptable. Adults have the responsibility to teach children to behave respectfully around other people. As adults, we need to know the difference and be teaching young people accordingly.

So, when a child misbehaves and acts out in a restaurant, disturbing everyone else trying to dine, it means something. When a child starts wailing or running around in church or during a special ceremony, it means something. When a child continually calls out to be heard and tugs at an adult's sleeve, while the adult is in the middle of a conversation, it means something.

Typically, these such behaviors mean that the child has not learned to respect others as they would like to be respected. This is not the child's fault. It's a teaching situation.

In other scenarios, there is no logical reason that the child needs to stop expressing their heart. In such situations, if an adult is impatient, they may not teach a quiet, compassionate lesson about respect. Instead, they may teach the child that their expressions are not worthy.

Children need to be encouraged to express themselves. They also need to be encouraged to recognize situations where it may be someone else's turn to express and our turn to be quiet and listen.

We all fare better when we can balance freely expressing and quietly listening. It's not easy. When a child has a story to share, an idea to explore, or a need to address, we adults must help them learn how to do so without stepping on others and without squelching the child's enthusiasm to express.

When children get fidgety, as may happen in church or some other scenario, we see some of them jump up and start running around, even talking loudly. Others sit quietly, though they may be bored to tears, and start playing with a quiet toy or reading a book.

Scolding a child in such an environment may not always be the best solution. The child may not yet understand concepts like decorum, or ceremony, or even listening. To respect others, we often need to inconvenience ourselves and leave the event with the child who is acting out or disturbing others.

Again, there is a teaching opportunity here. The manner and tonality with which we express to a child is far more impactful than that single event. To help youngsters grow in both knowledge and experience is important. It's best, however, when we can pull this off without making them feel as if they were failures or unworthy of being heard.

I recall not enjoying having to keep our "good" Sunday clothes on after church. We wanted to quickly shift into play clothes and get outside and be our rowdy selves. However, Mom wanted to teach us that we could not always control every bit of our schedules. We needed to stay neat and clean through Sunday dinner at a grandparent's home. Only after that did we get the "all clear" sign that we could go change our clothes and go out to play.

It didn't hurt us. It was not mandated in a manner that made us think we were bad. It was simply part of the teaching that we don't always make the rules, and that everything would be okay. We were learning respect and delayed gratification.

It's not very different than a parent teaching a child that they must make their bed and pick up their room before they can go out to play or go to a friend's house. The lesson learned is, "Yes." Yes, you can. However, there may be things to do first. Yes, we can talk and laugh and play. However, perhaps we need to be quiet for an hour first, while something else is happening. Yes, we can rough house, but not in public places.

Translating all of this into adulthood, we all likely know people who do not consistently behave with what we might consider socially acceptable decorum. However, those who *do* also tend to display respect for people in general. What we sometimes miss in the translation is that respectful behavior and language does not mean we cannot speak and laugh freely, as well.

Hesitation to express freely most frequently comes from our conditioning as we grew up. We *can* get our expressive comfortability back. As adults, we all have the power to regain the natural confidence and enthusiasm that we had as mere babes.

Six steps to express more freely:

1. <u>Release the chains of expectations</u>. Trying to live up to someone else's standards sets us up for failure or disappointment. We recognize that we should only try to control ourselves and how *we* behave or speak. So, don't relinquish your control choices to someone else's expectations.

2. <u>Accept that we'll goof up</u>. None of us is perfect, and that's okay. I talk very fast, so sometimes my words get all goofed up. I call it getting my "mords wixed." We can choose acceptance, rather than embarrassment.

3. <u>Go ahead and laugh</u>. I like to laugh at myself. It frees me from any pesky expectations or delusions of grandeur. Giggle or chuckle, guffaw or chortle, crack up or belly-laugh. Whether you howl, snort, titter, or whoop, laughter is healthy. Just don't make it at someone else's expense.

4. <u>Focus on your key point</u>. No script is needed, even if you feel shy. Know your intent. One word will do. If your intent is to express gratitude, for example, how you say it matters far less than you actually saying it. Share from your heart, and you'll do just fine.

5. <u>Select something positive or respectful to say</u>. Regardless of the topic at hand or how very deep you must dig to find something positive, this is worthy. It's easy to find negative things to say, but that makes us feel bad. You will love how empowering it is to express something positive.

6. <u>Share how you feel</u>. Start out a statement that may be perceived as controversial or critical with two important words: "I feel…" You are responding, not reacting, so no one "made" you feel that way. Express with compassion without pointing fingers.

**Tip:**
*If you would not be laughed at, be the first to laugh at yourself.*
-- Benjamin Franklin
American Author, Inventor & Diplomat
Founding Father of the United States

Rust Buster #10
## The Mandino Factor

> *Always do your best.*
> *What you plant now, you will harvest later.*
> -- Og Mandino  (1923 – 1996)
> American Author
> National Speakers Assn. Hall of Fame

Sometimes other people encourage us.  Other times, we can learn to encourage ourselves.  Then we can also add The Mandino Factor to our encouragement arsenal.

Using The Mandino Factor means we are harnessing past encouragement.  This means recalling encouragement given to us by someone in the past.  We can benefit whenever we need it in the present or future.

This encouragement factor is named for the famous best-selling author, Og Mandino.  He encouraged millions of people around the world with his books, from "The Greatest Salesman in the World" to "The Twelfth Angel."

Mandino had turned great tragedy and personal despair upside down and rebuilt his life.  As an inspiring author, he was gifted with the ability to share important themes and lessons in delightfully enriching parables.

While working in broadcast journalism, I was attending a funeral for a couple of friends who tragically lost their lives way too soon.  In the midst of hundreds of fellow mourners, I glimpsed a man I believed to be Og Mandino, my personal favorite author.

Later, I was able to approach Og and his wife, Bette. I shared with them how personally touched I had been by his work.

Bless their hearts! They had spied me in the crowd, also, and had been making their way toward me.

Humbling barely begins to describe the feeling I had upon learning that *they* considered themselves to be fans of *mine*. We quickly turned our mutual admiration society "fanship" into friendship.

When I later did a half-hour television interview program with them, Bette shared it was the first time she'd been included in Og's spotlight. She was lovely, and I assured her I wouldn't have considered leaving her out.

As our friendship grew, I enjoyed visiting them in their home. (Og's office and library could have been a museum. Bette's Santa Claus collection was unforgettable.)

These two beautiful human beings openly encouraged my speaking and writing skills. They'd loved my various documentaries, news programs, and specials, and they believed I most assuredly had at least a book or two in me.

Promoting his books, Og Mandino had become active with the National Speakers Association. His gentle and humble speaking style was captivating.

He encouraged me to follow in his footsteps, saying that I was more motivating for people than I realized. He virtually insisted that I join him as a professional member of the NSA myself. (Yes, thanks to him, I did so for more than twenty years.)

Og and Bette Mandino were championing me. Me! What??!!? I didn't want to let them down. When someone believes strongly in us, and they take the time and personal effort to tell us so, the encouragement is powerful.

Even today, when I sit down to write, I can almost see Og Mandino grinning at me. When I stand up to speak publicly, I can almost hear his gentle, but steadfastly encouraging words. "You can do it. You need to do this. People need you."

I share this particular story with you because we all likely have people like this who have been in our lives! We know their hearts. We have felt the warmth of their encouragement. We have basked in the grace of their confidence. We have tried harder because they told us we could do it. They are our Og Mandinos.

These people may no longer be part of our lives or even still be alive on this earth. Yet, we can learn to recall the essence of those gifts they shared with us.

## Harnessing past encouragement is the power behind The Mandino Factor.

Born Augustine Mandino on December 12, 1923, Og Mandino passed away on September 3, 1996. To me, his is a legacy of hope, persistency, and encouragement. I remember his lessons. His words. His confidence. His encouragement. They are powerful recollections.

I can harness the positive power by remembering. So can *you*.

Perhaps there was a family member. Maybe it was a teacher or a coach. A neighbor or friend. It could have been a boss or co-worker. A pastor. A clerk in a store. The possibilities for remembering something encouraging that was done or said for us are endless. We simply need to open our minds and hearts to remember.

Think back to a time when someone did something or said something to give you that "can-do" confidence. That belief in yourself to "go for it." That encouragement to keep on keeping on.

Remember how they made you feel. Each and every time you do this, you will be harnessing their encouragement all over again. You are harnessing The Mandino Factor for yourself.

Og Mandino with the author, 1992

**Tip:**

*I love the light for it shows me the way,*
*yet I endure the darkness because it shows me the stars.*
-- Og Mandino  (1923 – 1996)
American Author
National Speakers Assn. Hall of Fame

Rust Buster #11
## Unleash Your Inner Encourager

*You yourself, as much as anybody in the entire universe,*
*deserve your love and affection.*
-- Gautama Buddha (c.563 - c.483 BC)
Monk on whose teachings
Buddhism was founded

## Our value does not diminish because of someone else's inability to see our worth.

Try to remember that some of these folks are so busy patting themselves on the back that they would struggle to see value in someone else. They know that they know everything worth knowing, and we know nothing. Riiight!

Simply smile. Leave them to be what they want. They will not sincerely encourage us or anyone else.

*To love oneself is the beginning of a life-long romance.*
-- Oscar Wilde (1854 – 1900)
Irish Poet and Playwright

Self-encouragement is a powerful tool. To use it most effectively, we must first learn to develop this resource. Otherwise, in our time of need, our confidence could feel too depleted to enable us to stir our inner Encourager.

Self-help comes in many forms. The same is true of self-encouragement. Let's look at 10 highly effective ways to encourage ourselves.

## #1 – Reject Pity Party Invitations
I promised we'd look at this again, because it is vital. Negative attitudes are highly contagious. When Life goes awry, the negative whirlpool can sweep us along in its undertow.

If someone near us is ranting and raving or ragging nastily about someone, choose not to join the attack. If possible, put some physical distance between yourself and the pouting party, even if just for a few minutes. Think of it as being a bit like road rage or fights on the football field. It takes two people to escalate rage. It's easy to react "in kind" to negativity. It takes courage to walk away.

You are stronger than you may believe. Walking away prevents us from discouraging ourselves, which has the natural reverse effect of being encouraging.

## #2 – Keep an Encouragement Inventory
We often receive uplifting messages or see positively moving or meaningful videos. This happens through email and social media accounts regularly. Save these precious items. Store them in a place that's easy for you to access. They can work wonders at times when we may feel alone or discouraged.

I love reading books that inspire me to highlight phrases or lines that I find particularly impactful. Or I turn down corners of pages that I want to refer to later.

The same is true of uplifting quotations. I've kept collections of great quotations since I was a child and first learned to read. Some I categorized by their themes.

However, before personal computers, I gleefully had folders and boxes filled with favorite sayings that I randomly jotted down and tucked in my folders. They always proved powerful for self-encouragement when I needed a boost.

Many of us find great encouragement in favorite Bible verses. Or perhaps certain songs regularly seem to give you a lift. Write down the things that encourage you.

All that matters is preparing this Inventory of Encouragement when we *don't* need it. Then it's ready at our fingertips when we *do*.

### #3 – Grow Daily
We all have different skills. Yet, no matter how good we may be at a particular thing, we need to practice, improve, stretch, and polish. The more we work at our skills, the more confident we become. Improving ourselves is highly self-encouraging.

I recall reading that Frank Sinatra, ol' Blue Eyes himself, continued to work with a vocal coach his entire life. Wow! With hundreds of albums and countless live performances, it would have seemed that this crooner extraordinaire surely didn't need to keep studying and polishing his craft.

Au contraire! We all need to invest time and attention to becoming the best we can be. If we need to work on skills we already possess, then most assuredly we also improve when we work on areas in which we *know* we need improvement. Poof! Instant self-encouragement!

### #4 – Talk Positively to Yourself

We all talk to ourselves unconsciously anyway. Now we want to train our self-talk to be positive. Typically, our messages to ourselves happen silently. On the other hand, I know I am not alone when I say that on more than one occasion, I have coached myself sternly and loudly when I am struggling mightily with something. These are deliberate pep talks with positive purpose.

"I can do it!" "I've got this!" "I am worthy!" This is all very healthy.

Try writing down positive statements about yourself. Start simply. There is no need to feel profound in any way. Try it.

I am kind.
I genuinely care about others.
I respect people.
I am tolerant.
I am open-minded.

Keep your list growing. Store it where you can access it readily. Start and end each day reading your list, whether it contains just a few phrases or many dozens. In fact, it can help sometimes if we try selecting one of our items each day. That phrase or statement will get our special attention that day.

For example, "I am tolerant" was a powerful reminder for me when political divisiveness seemed to be making people talk horribly and treat each other most meanly. "I am tolerant" became a vital tool to help me reach out to people in positive ways, rather than rudely scathing attacks or responses. We are claiming and reinforcing the positive.

By stating and restating a positive observation about ourselves, we strengthen it.  Bit by bit, day by day, the positives squelch out our negatives by weakening them.  Thus, our positive self-talk is highly self-encouraging both on short-term and long-term levels.

### #5 - Reboot

We reboot our computers when the screen freezes.  We reboot televisions when a picture or connection goes haywire.  Why not learn how to reboot our own enthusiasm?

Sometimes things become a little more than just challenging.  We shut down.  Ah-hah!  Time for a reboot.

I'm not saying it's always easy.  In fact, rebooting our enthusiasm and staying positive can be extremely difficult.  I worked hard at becoming a positive person.  After a while, I didn't even realize it had happened.

I recall reading an article in "USA Today" that said less than one percent of the U.S. population wakes up happy every day.  Well, I knew I was strange, but I hadn't realized just how strange.  I wake up happy every day.  I guess there are far worse categories in which we could land in the 1 percent group.

In the spirit of transparency, I must acknowledge that I didn't always wake up happy.  Like most of us, I sometimes awoke with crazy stress over what had been troubling me.  I sometimes awoke with a feeling of fear or even dread over what loomed ahead of me on a given day.

However, I learned to reboot.  We *can* shut down, let it all go, and start fresh and positive the next day.

None of us must wake up with daily negative thoughts. When we get down on ourselves, we need to reboot. We can deliver some solid, positive self-talk. We can re-read our positive self-statements, check out a positive video, or chat with an encouraging friend.

**Rebooting our enthusiasm is like deciding to become our own best coach, rather than our own worst enemy.**

Rebooting lets us refocus on positive, rather than wallowing in negatives or self-pity. We can all do it. We all *need* to do it sometimes. Turn the page. Reboot.

### #6 – Don't Get Stuck in a Rut

Changing it up can be very refreshing, not to mention a great self-encouragement tool. This doesn't mean you have to make any massive changes at all. For example, there is no need to change jobs, drop a girlfriend, or trade in your car.

Try a couple simple changes. Drive a different route to work. Wear a new, unexpected color. Dine in a different restaurant. Call a friend or family member you haven't spoken with in a while… just to say, "Hi!" Watch a TV show you didn't previously know. Eat a soup variety you haven't tasted in years.

Some of the smallest changes can measurably boost our morale. We are creatures of habit. While routine helps us maintain persistency, it can also get us stuck in ruts.

**Just because we *should* know better
doesn't mean we *do*.**

Once we prove to ourselves that we can make little changes without disrupting our universe, we start to dare to believe in ourselves more. We are encouraging ourselves to branch out, to stretch, and to grow.

Remember, changing routines does not need to be dramatic. Bit by bit we grow. Two steps forward with one step back is still forward motion. Slow progress is still progress. Even a touch of progress is very self-encouraging.

### #7 – Tap into Role Models
Choose positive role models and emulate the traits and behaviors you most admire. As you learn their philosophies, you may well find more like-minded people. We can't always have our role models nearby to encourage us, but we can learn to tap into the encouragement they provide us even when they are not around.

Find their blogs or posts on social media sites like Facebook or LinkedIn. Read them often. Re-read them. You may find books they've written. Or autobiographies or biographies.

Learning from people we respect is healthy. Far too often we get in a habit of reading, watching, or listening to junk… just because we are used to doing it. Following people we respect motivates, inspires, and encourages us. We are tapping into what makes great people tick. We are applying "The Mandino Factor" to our ability to encourage ourselves.

### #8 – Meaning Matters

Whenever we feel a purpose in our lives, we perform better. This becomes more pronounced when that purpose is selfless. When we pursue goals that benefit others, that selfless activity adds even greater meaning.

Remember the sage remarks about feeling bad because I had no shoes until I met the man who had no feet? That's perspective. That's how meaning makes Life matter. We rarely understand why bad things happen to good people. It's hard to find meaning in situations that appear utterly senseless. Why do these things happen?

We looked at this earlier, and I wish I had answers. I wish anyone did. While answers remain elusive, we can find value and meaning even when it's hard to see.

When someone gets hurt or dies, we are reminded to hug those we love a little closer. When raging fires wipe out neighborhoods, we may take steps to back up vital documents and family photographs on "the cloud." We count our blessings. We donate to relief funds. We say our prayers. We stop taking things for granted… even if only temporarily.

## It bears repeating…
## only storms make us appreciate fair weather.

We can transfer these lessons in perspective to every aspect of our lives. For example, if I am frustrated with my job, I can learn to be thankful to have a job. If I am annoyed with my spouse, I can remember that he will love and stand by me in the toughest times.

When we feel down in the dumps, without hope, we can find meaning in the fact that somewhere, sometime, someone looked up to us or appreciated us or needed us… even when we may not have known it.

### #9 – Savor the Rewards

When we seek the ability to encourage ourselves, we can get side-tracked, frustrated, and "blurry-visioned" (if that's an expression). We can motivate and encourage ourselves with little rewards along the way. These give us things to look forward to during struggles.

Let's say that we have been working hard at completing a project. Plan a reward. When you get through items A, B, and C, you get the reward. That reward could be a dish of ice cream, an hour of video games, a favorite TV show, or a soak in a hot bath.

Just remember to make rewards proportionate with the tasks or accomplishments. If I mowed the lawn, rewarding myself with a trip to Aruba would be outlandishly goofy. But I can look forward to enjoying a fruity ice bar from the freezer.

If I finished folding laundry and cleaning the house, I would be off-base to reward myself with a thousand-dollar shopping spree at the mall. I could get that pepperoni pizza delivered, instead of making dinner.

Rewarding ourselves not only gives us things to look forward to, but it acknowledges what we have accomplished. It encourages us.

Sometimes these are long-term accomplishments. Other times, we have completed an intermediary or mundane task.

We don't need *others* to see what we have done. But we do score in the self-encouragement arena when *we* recognize our own progress.

We use rewards to train a new puppy. Eventually, we transition the pup to relishing an "Atta-boy" pat on the head instead of bites of biscuits. Surely, we can learn to reward ourselves with a few DIY pats on the back, too!

## #10 – Refresh and Renew

Have you ever felt so tired that nothing seemed to flow exactly as it should? I think this happens to all of us from time to time. We push and push and push ourselves so hard that we become physically, mentally, emotionally, and spiritually exhausted.

Schedule time for renewal. This keeps us more balanced. Start with several nights of good sleep. Don't watch TV or go out. Simply relax. Turn in early. Read some of those meaningful items from your Encouragement Inventory. Give yourself some of that positive, healing, restful self-talk. Play soft, relaxing music perhaps.

Whatever works for you is fine. Let positive, healing, relaxing thoughts and images flow from the top of your head to the tips of your toes. Allowing ourselves time to renew and refresh opens our hearts and minds, which is extremely self-encouraging.

**Tip:** Glean great lessons in self-encouragement from sources that teach us to not just survive, but to thrive! It was Christopher Robin in "Winnie the Pooh" who said, "Always remember you are braver than you believe, stronger than you seem, and smarter than you think."

Rust Buster #12
# Encourager Extraordinaire

Different things inspire different people. One gal gushes
enthusiastically about the guy in the jacked up pick-up truck.
The driver revs the engine to a throaty growl, as if he's the
sexiest thing on earth. She swoons.

Her girlfriend retorts, "Hah! That yahoo is merely showing
his lack of confidence... and likely something else!" She
tosses her head back and laughs. Different strokes.

To become an Encourager isn't as difficult as we might think.
Having more Encouragers in this world is more important
than we might think. How to become one or become an even
better one involves a few basics.


1. <u>Become aware of what encourages you</u>. Use that
information to encourage others. We are not all encouraged
by the same things, but sharing and trying to encourage are
important. For example, I say, "Merry Christmas" because it's
an expression of love and sharing and celebration in my faith.
The person to whom I said it may or may not be of my faith,
but my message is sincere and should not ever be construed as
an insult to *any* recipient, even if they happen to be an atheist.
If someone says, "Happy Hanukah" to me it does not mean
they don't realize that I am not Jewish. It means they are
sharing their happy spirit with me. Return the positive
gesture... with a smile!

2. <u>See something, say something</u>. This is not just airport
security protocol. This is Life. When we see something good
or positive that someone has done, tell them. Tell everyone!
Remember, we all need "Atta boys!" Even if someone simply
looks good on a particular day, due to a color they are

wearing or some attention they've paid to their hair, compliment them genuinely.

3. <u>To start out, decide to be an Encourager three times a day</u>. Each of us can find three things each day which warrant a positive comment, a sincere compliment, or a boosting word. Use details and specifics when you compliment or praise someone. That's like using someone's name. This adds validity and value to your words.

4. <u>Take extra care around family, friends, your spouse, and other loved ones</u>. Observe more regularly. Share your appreciation. It is so terribly easy to take those closest to us for granted. The same often applies to our co-workers, because we see them every day.

5. <u>Use email and social media for positive good</u>. Respond thoughtfully to three postings each time you go to your social media sites. Send people thoughtful emails, not the messages begging for them to copy & paste or forward to everyone they know. If I did that for each that I get, it could take hours. Post something meaningful, and friends will pass it forward.

6. <u>When someone has been an Encourager for you, tell them what they did or said</u>. Share with them how it mattered and made a difference for you. Apply the Attitude of Gratitude.

7. <u>Remember that old-fashioned face-to-face visits and conversations are still wonderfully appreciated</u>. It's special to look people in the eyes when we share. This also lets them see you are genuinely listening to them.

8. <u>Send a hand-written note or greeting card to someone from time to time</u>. It shows an extra level of care and effort was taken and reflects your sincerity.

9. <u>Consciously look to see what may be good and right in an idea someone shares</u>. Try not to seek and spew over what may be wrong. Seek out positive values and pass them on without judgment.

10. <u>Smile and laugh more</u>. And mean it.

If you've read any of my other works, even my cookbooks, you know that I am very keen on Keeping It Super Simple. This philosophy applies to the paths we follow to surround ourselves with encouraging people and to become better Encouragers, too.

The steps I must follow may lead me on a long and twisted path. Or up and down some steep terrain. Your path may be far smoother. You may be on a super highway! Or not.

With easing your path in mind, following are some Super Simple steps to help us all become what I call Encouragers Extraordinaire! Just take the steps *you* need and in any order that suits you. Gleefully skip items that don't apply or that you've already mastered. Each one could be developed as its own chapter, so choose what you want and enjoy the journey.

Be gentle with yourself and others, demonstrating the true strength in being gentle.

When someone stumbles, help them learn and discover solutions.

Display a genuinely positive attitude.

Listen sincerely with genuine interest.

Remain trustworthy.

Boost someone's morale by sharing a sincere "Good job" acknowledgement.

Choose to be a good role model.

Be the energy and light you would like to see in your world.

Keep the faith and let your faith blossom as a safe, loving place for others.

Become a beacon of hope by telling someone why you believe in them and their abilities.

Build others' confidence up by reminding them of what they are doing right.

Guide people to develop the skills they need to reach their goals.

Instruct others by giving them specific steps that can help them do better.

Acknowledge the value in someone else's goals, even when they aren't shared by you.

Empower others by helping them learn to solve problems.

Behave in consistent, persistent, and positive ways.

Seek and find the potential in other people; acknowledge it out loud to them.

See and appreciate strength and talent in others.

Cheer others on to victory.

Put the fun in fundamental, to help others see the value in "staying the course."

Surround yourself with people who calm you and become a calming influence for others.

Heal others by loving even the seemingly unlovable.

Teach others to recognize challenges as stepping stones, not stumbling blocks.

Develop "Can Do" thinking and expressions.

Lead by positive example.

Speak kindly and honestly, using encouraging words.

Make less judgmental comments.

Squelch all urges to participate in "Stinking Thinking."

Deliver criticism in a compassionate manner that demonstrates you believe the person can do better.

Observe efforts and offer sincere praise for actual achievements, no matter how slight.

Claim responsibility for your choices and decisions. No passing the buck.

Admit mistakes, sincerely apologize, and work to make amends.

Show respect for other's schedules by not disrupting their plans or assigning higher values to your priorities.

Practice random acts of kindness.

Share or give proper credit to others for successes.

Openly learn from others and let them know how they have mattered to you.

Vow not to permit fear to halt your progress, and help others overcome fears.

Suggest trying new techniques and approaches.

Stress the fun and adventure in reaching beyond our comfort zones.

Open your mind to trying new ways to get a task completed and set that example.

Teach others to pace themselves and to organize the inevitable chaos.

Make and honor commitments.

Encourage people to not compromise themselves or their values.

Help others behave in ways that earn respect and admiration.

Brighten a room by entering it.

When I first started writing non-fiction, I knew I wanted to help lift people. I wanted to validate independent thinking. I hoped to encourage people to believe in themselves. Sure, I am just one person, but I wanted to quietly make some noise, if that makes sense.

That was the inspiration for my publishing company name. Quiet Thunder. Publishing on the "QT," as it were. By becoming Encouragers and Encouragers Extraordinaire, we can all make a little quiet (or not so quiet) noise!

**Tip:**

*Do you want to know who you are? Don't ask. Act!*
*Action will delineate and define you.*
-- Thomas Jefferson (1743 - 1826)
3rd United States President
American Founding Father
Author of Declaration of Independence

Photo Credit: Nicholas Sampson

Rust Buster #13
# Encourage Your Way to Success

*Get going. Move forward. Aim high. Plan a takeoff. Don't just sit on the runway and hope someone will come along and push the airplane. It simply won't happen.*
*Change your attitude and gain some altitude.*
-- Donald J. Trump  (1946 - )
45th President of the United States

We can triumph in all aspects of life. I want you to relish your family and relationships. I want you to thrive in your job and activities. I want you to flourish in your church and community. Succeed in achieving happiness and balance in your faith, family, and work, and I believe you will be enjoying the greatest achievements.

Remember that part of moving forward often involves stumbling a few steps back. None of us is perfect. In order to encourage our way to achieving our goals, we likely need a little polishing.

Some of these things we could consider basics, although we may need a little reminding now and then. For example, my husband loves to say, "God gave you two ears and one mouth." That means I should listen more than I speak. All true. Several gal pals of mine note that our voices seem to be at a frequency that is incomprehensible to our husbands. Even when they look at us straight in the eye as we ask a question, we can't be sure they heard a word we said. I have learned to request a physical sign.... Nodding or shaking of the head... to let me know there is acknowledgement that I spoke and was heard.

As comical as this might sound, if someone feels ignored and unheard by us, we have a lot of growing to do. As annoying as it may be to pay attention to someone else, it's an important part of encouraging your way to achieving your goals.

Another basic is to lift people up, rather than put them down. Use uplifting words, rather than sneers, scoffing faces, or what I call "Nasty-grams." Consider the old expression to "turn that frown upside down." We move closer to achieving our personal and professional aspirations when we become skilled at finding the silver linings in the storm clouds. A smile takes us a mile… and more.

Here comes a tough basic for some people. Okay, I'll say it. A tough basic, particularly for those who might be deemed "Control Freaks," is to respect another person's time, worth, and sensibility. Nothing is quite as professionally or personally demeaning as having someone *else* repeatedly set priorities for *us*.

This usually entails forcing us to break commitments, change plans, and basically feel rather off balance much of the time. Respect is a big one, and it needs to be a two-way street.

**There's also nothing quite as demoralizing as working or living with someone who seems bent on being against us.**

They don't open doors; they slam them. They don't suggest stepping stones or building blocks. Instead, they repeatedly attempt to block our path and goals.

Sometimes folks do this out of their own insecurity. Other times they are not paying attention.

Regardless, as people who strive to encourage and work toward our achievement goals, we know that we do not want to be known as people who merely resist, resist, resist simply to block someone's way. Persist, persist, persist? Yes. Assist, assist, assist is good, too.

Another tremendous basic skill to best encourage our way to success involves learning to respond, rather than react. We've likely heard this many times and in many ways. Actuality is like that. Bar room brawls do not hail from logical, thoughtful places. They erupt purely from emotionally reactionary scenarios. We can do better. And we must.

Throughout our days we may encounter many situations in which someone is reaching for a goal, struggling to develop a good habit or break a bad one, or otherwise striving for success. We hurt no one when we encourage them to keep on keeping on, to not give up, to recognize how far they've come. That very simply improves life for everyone.

*My mother drew a distinction between achievement and success.*
*She said that achievement is the knowledge*
*that you have studied and worked hard*
*and done the best that is in you.*
*Success is being praised by others.*
*That is nice but not as important or satisfying.*
*Always aim for achievement and forget about success.*
-- Helen Hayes  (1900 – 1993)
American Actress

If we are in any sort of management or supervisory capacity, we can be particularly impactful on the total achievement and success of our company by boosting the morale of our team. Recognize folks who've hit a goal or who went the extra mile for someone. Skip the standard email and opt to say, "Good job" right to someone's face. Take a little time to recognize and even celebrate work anniversaries. Force the workaholics away from their desks to enjoy a teambuilding lunch regularly with the group.

Be aware if a person is struggling through a personal situation or may need more time off than they have earned. Perhaps others could donate some of their earned hours or personal time. Getting a little creative involves paying attention first to identify opportunities to develop some encouraging twists.

Whatever we are doing in our professional or personal lives, we all achieve more when we feel encouraged and we are encouraging to others. That's like a natural law.

## Respecting, understanding, and appreciating people makes us better people.

Those who lack empathy with others don't really "get" that concept. They cannot imagine what it would be like to walk a mile in someone else's shoes, nor do they want to try to understand.

These Discouragers are not the folks with whom we want to surround ourselves. We want to be with people who see our strengths and weaknesses and choose to appreciate and encourage us.

They like people and are open and honest about it. They are emotionally healthy, even though Life is far from perfect.

They value us as individuals, and we feel it. We see it. We hear it. They are the Encouragers.

## We want to be with Encouragers, and we want to be like them.

When we choose to live openly and vulnerably, we need a great deal of courage. As my General Manager, David Zamichow, put it when I first started in television news broadcasting, "The higher you go, the more sharks will be circling." Well said.

Yet, the courageous push onward, and they lift others, encouraging them to do and be the best they can be. Their Attitude of Gratitude can be awe-inspiring. When we see this behavior, this tone, this encouragement in others, we respect it deeply.

Their courage gives us courage. Their encouragement makes us want to encourage others, too. They connect. They lead. They mentor. They inspire.

Discouragers are dream stealers. They often believe that the only way to succeed is to push other people down. They don't understand they are covered with rust.

Now we can be like the Tin Man in "The Wizard of Oz." We have lots of Rust Busters in our little oil cans.

# Encouragement

Whether Discouragers like it or not, Encouragers will persist in squirting a little spritz of hope, confidence, and support into the darkest, rustiest corners. We won't allow Discouragers to define a tiny box in which we must fit.

We will determine who we are and will be, and fellow Encouragers will be there to lift us.

**Tip:** Conrad Hilton, the great American hotelier who lived from 1887 to 1979 pulled no punches when he said, "Achievement seems to be connected with action. Successful men and women keep moving. They make mistakes, but they don't quit."

Rust Buster #14
# Organize the Chaos

Whether we like it or not, chaos seems to be a great part of our lives. We just don't want to let it get out of control.

When teaching public speaking, I'd often quip to the students that those nervous butterflies in their stomachs are perfectly natural. Feeling nervous reveals that we do not want to fail. We do not want to disappoint or let our audience down.

If someone with whom I was about to be on a theatre stage with in a comedy or musical said they weren't nervous, I was taken aback. To me that revealed that they may well lack focus and concentration. If something went wrong during the production, we might not be able to count on any recovery help from them.

I believe that each audience matters and matters deeply. I respect them. I want them to receive just as stirring and rousing a performance as the opening night audience got. To me, that is important. So, sure, I am nervous. I care.

To prove to a theatre cast I was directing that they all had the power to deliver excellence, I'd have them "mock through" the entire play without scripts after the first read-through.

Okay, it became a *very* short show. But from just one read-through every person knew how their character fit in with everyone else's and the start-to-finish storyline. This gave great confidence that they could get through the show successfully, regardless of what chaos happened, particularly since they'd have plenty of rehearsal time before they were truly put to the test.

Embrace the nervous butterflies in your stomach. Put in the work so you can have confidence in yourself. You are training the butterflies.

## All we need to do
## is get those nervous butterflies in our stomachs
## flying in formation.

Another great trick to organize the chaos is to maintain written "To Do" lists. I've got the "Have to Do," "Need to Do," and "Want to Do" varieties. Yes, I love crossing things off the lists! Organization is like having a plan and working that plan.

My Mom sets the pace for us in this regard and many others. She's always in motion. I can remember as a child, we three kids were in the back seat as Dad drove, but Mom was always busily working on projects.

She used every possible minute to get things done. Sometimes she might be snapping green bean we'd picked in our garden, or she'd be writing letters or cards, or planning menus for some holiday gathering.

Naturally, when she wasn't stuck in a car, she was always busy, too. In whatever minutes we had left before a departure time, she would be actively working… cleaning the kitchen, vacuuming, ironing, sewing, cooking, whatever. Time management was a tough challenge, but she was never bored.

Even now, with my Mother in her 89th year, she is very active. To say Mom keeps busy is an understatement.

She's the floor representative for her sixth floor in the independent living apartment complex where she lives, manages the greeting card shop, swims regularly, sings in concerts with the big Fun Chorus, goes to church weekly, and manages all her various social calendar items, such as bridge games and regular lunch and dinner groups. And more.

She's a marvel. Her example shows that having meaning and purpose each day keeps us going. Having a calendar and "To Do" lists keeps us organized.

We offspring learned work ethic from our parents. As students, we always took a full load of classes and maintained high levels of involvement in school, church, and community activities and organizations. Plus, we had responsibilities at home.

We learned commitment. Respect. Teamwork.

To this day I do not ever recall having five minutes when I felt even close to being bored. No way! There's never any time to be bored.

On the other hand, zooming through our days with too much to do can challenge our time management abilities. This adds stress to an already stressful life.

If we practice good time management, we are far less vulnerable to discouragement. Think about it. When we suffer with far too many items on our "To Do" lists, we stress out. When we see items being crossed off upon completion, we become encouraged and energized. Think of time management as a powerful tool toward stress management.

I am as guilty as anyone else of slipping up in the time management arena. However, I learned how to prioritize, which became a superb stress reducer.

Remember... not everything belongs on our "Have to Do" list. Perhaps someone else can help with something on the list. Perhaps some items can be delayed or even dropped.

For example, I usually try to do too much in preparing to host holiday parties. I learned to give myself a time deadline. Let's say 3 o'clock. If I hadn't started a recipe by that time, it was off the menu. Period. If I hadn't put up some particular decorations, then it wasn't happening. Period. This forced me to put my "To Do" items in order of actual importance.

I apply the same time rules each day to accomplish the most vital tasks. I make a point to stop with a large enough time window to be ready to depart for work or serve dinner or whatever, without adding extra stress for trying to accomplish two or three extra things.

By adhering to my "Rule of the Deadline," I de-stress myself. Give it a try. It's very empowering. Empowerment is very encouraging. This is a learned skill. It's one we learn after driving ourselves crazy enough times by piling on extra time pressures.

**Tip:**

*Never let the odds keep you from doing*
*what you know in your heart you were meant to do.*
    -- H. Jackson Brown, Jr. (1940 - )
    American Author

Bonus Rust Buster #15

# Righteous Expressions

When we seek encouraging words, we learn quickly to not seek them from the Discouragers in our midst. They have most likely been discouraged throughout their lives. They have built-up fears. They lack confidence, even when they feign an air of confidence or even superiority.

We may love them, but we can't help them until we feel confident that we have become or are becoming Encouragers Extraordinaire. Then, not only can't they burst our bubble, but we may actually be skilled enough to bring them into the lighter, brighter, happier world of encouragement.

We start now by safeguarding our goals and dreams from Discouragers. We learn to only talk about goals and dreams with the most supportive people we know.

Meanwhile, we learn to tune out Discouragers by lowering the volume they emit. We can't always physically disengage, but we can learn to mentally not let them crush our hopes and dreams. Sometimes all it takes is a basic evaluation of what they command... er, uh, say.

When feeling overwhelmed by a Discourager, ask yourself a few questions. If we do as they suggest, will we be more apt to succeed or achieve our goals? Does what they say hold validity? Are they criticizing or blocking or sincerely trying to provide us with guidance to succeed?

Surround yourself with Encouragers. Find like-minded friends. Don't spend time worrying about people who have built walls or closed their minds to possibilities that you still see.

There are plenty of church and civic organizations that do positive things. So, if you fear you'll be alone, think again. Get involved in a good church or a good cause, and you will also be getting to know other positive people.

Also, take the time to support the dreams and goals of other people. Remember, you are or are becoming an Encourager. People gravitate to possibility thinkers. That creates win-win scenarios all day long.

Again, I emphasize the importance of gathering positive, encouraging words and thoughts around you. We need a lot of ammunition to insulate ourselves from Discouragers.

Life is a struggle. Regardless of what you're struggling with, it helps to hear words of encouragement that remind us that we all take knocks in Life, but the best things in Life often come through the door of persistence.

Whether you've just had another setback chasing your dreams, been rejected by someone you care about, faced tragedy, or you're just feeling drained from the ups and downs of this journey we call Life, remember that things can turn around in an instant. All we must do is keep moving forward, even when it feels like it would be easier to lay down and give up.

No matter what you're going through, here are some encouraging quotes that will hopefully give you a little boost from time to time and get your Encouragement Inventory growing. Many of these quotes come from individuals who have achieved incredible success in life, and just like you, they had low points where everything felt hopeless.

*Focus on remedies, not faults.*
-- Jack Nicklaus  (1940 - )
American Professional Golfer


*If you fell down yesterday, stand up today.*
-- H.G. Wells  (1866 – 1946)
English Novelist, Historian & Journalist


*Keep your eyes on the stars and your feet on the ground.*
-- Theodore Roosevelt  (1858 – 1919)
26th President of the United States


*Do your work with your whole heart, and you will succeed.*
*There's so little competition.*
-- Elbert Hubbard  (1856 – 1915)
American Writer & Philosopher


*The most effective way to do it, is to do it.*
-- Amelia Earhart  (1897 – 1937)
American Aviation Pioneer


*The harder the conflict, the more glorious the triumph.*
-- Thomas Paine  (1737 – 1809)
English-born American Political Activist


*If the wind will not serve, take to the oars.*
-- Latin Proverb

*Our greatest glory is not in never falling,*
*but in rising every time we fall.*
-- Confucius  (551 – 479 BC)
Chinese Teacher, Politician & Philosopher

*Destiny is not a matter of chance, it is a matter of choice.*
*It is not a thing to be waited for, it is a thing to be achieved.*
-- William Jennings Bryan  (1860 – 1925)
American Orator & Politician

*To reach a great height a person needs to have great depth.*
-- Anonymous

*In the confrontation between the stream and the rock, the stream*
*always wins – not through strength but by perseverance.*
-- H. Jackson Brown, Jr.  (1940 - )
American Author

*My great concern is not whether you have failed,*
*but whether you are content with your failure.*
– Abraham Lincoln  (1809 – 1865)
16th President of the United States

*The difference between the impossible and the possible*
*lies in a person's determination.*
-- Tommy Lasorda  (1927 - )
American MLB Player & Manager

*A leader, once convinced that a particular course of action is the right one, must… be undaunted when the going gets tough.*
-- Ronald Reagan  (1911 – 2004)
40th President of the United States


*The moment you doubt whether you can fly,*
*you cease forever to be able to do it.*
-- J. M. Barrie  (1860 – 1937)
Scottish Novelist & Playwright
From "Peter Pan"


*Twenty years from now you will be more disappointed by the things you didn't do than by the ones you did do.  So throw off the bowlines.  Sail away from the safe harbor.  Catch the trade winds in your sail. Explore. Dream. Discover.*
– Mark Twain (Pen name)
Samuel Clemens  (1835 – 1910)
American Writer, Humorist & Lecturer


## Do what you can, where you are, with what you have.


*It's not the years in your life that count.  It's the life in your years.*
– Abraham Lincoln  (1809 – 1865)
16th President of the United States


*You can't use up creativity.  The more you use it, the more you have.*
– Maya Angelou  (1928 – 2014)
American Poet & Civil Rights Activist

# Encouragement

*The two most important days in your life are the day you are born and the day you find out why.*
– Mark Twain (Pen name)
Samuel Clemens  (1835 – 1910)
American Writer, Humorist & Lecturer


*Whether you think you can or think you can't, you are right.*
–Henry Ford   (1863 – 1947)
American Business Magnate


*There are no traffic jams along the extra mile.*
– Roger Staubach  (1942 -  )
American NFL Quarterback


*There is only one way to avoid criticism.*
*Do nothing, say nothing, and be nothing.*
– Aristotle  (384 – 322 BC)
Greek Philosopher & Scientist


*Remember that not getting what you want is sometimes a wonderful stroke of luck.*
– The Dalai Lama
Tibetan Spiritual Leader
1st was Pema Dorje (1391 – 1474)


*Winning isn't everything, but wanting to win is.*
– Vince Lombardi  (1913 – 1970)
American NFL Player, Coach & Executive

*I hated every minute of training, but I said, "Don't quit. Suffer now, and live the rest of your life as a champion."*
-- Muhammad Ali (1942 – 2016)
Born Cassius Clay, Jr.
American World Boxing Champion


*It is never too late to be what you might have been.*
– George Eliot  (Pen Name)
Mary Anne Evans (1819 – 1880)
English Novelist, Poet & Journalist


*Every strike brings me closer to the next home run.*
– Babe Ruth  (1895 – 1948)
American Pro Baseball Player


*One man with courage makes a majority.*
– Andrew Jackson  (1767 – 1845)
7th President of the United States


*Champions keep playing until they get it right.*
– Billie Jean King  (1943 -  )
American Pro Tennis Player; #1 in World


*It is not what you do for your children,
but what you have taught them to do for themselves
that will make them successful human beings.*
– Ann Landers  (Pen name 1943 – 2002)
Created by Chicago Sun-Times Advice
Columnist Ruth Crowley;
Esther Lederer from 1955

*Wisdom is the reward you get for a lifetime of listening
when you'd have preferred to talk.*
– Doug Larson  (1926 – 2017)
Columnist and Editor


*You must never be fearful about what you are doing when it is right.*
-- Rosa Parks (1913 – 2005)
American Civil Rights Activist


*It always seems impossible until it is done.*
-- Nelson Mandela (1918 – 1999)
President of South Africa (1994 – 1999)
Anti-Apartheid Leader & Philanthropist


*Trust yourself.  You know more than you think you do.*
-- Dr. Benjamin Spock  (1903 – 1998)
American Pediatrician & Author


**It doesn't matter how slowly you go
as long as you do not stop.**


*Fight one more round.  When your arms are so tired that you can
hardly lift your hands to come on guard, fight one more round.
When your nose is bleeding and your eyes are black and you are so
tired that you wish your opponent would crack you one on the jaw
and put you to sleep, fight one more round – remembering that the
man who always fights one more round is never whipped.*
-- James Corbett (1866 – 1933)
American Boxer & World Champion

*Never tell people how to do things. Tell them what to do and they will surprise you with their ingenuity.*
-- George S. Patton, Jr.  (1885 – 1945)
United States Army General

*I consider my ability to arouse enthusiasm among men the greatest asset I possess. The way to develop the best that is in a man is by appreciation and encouragement.*
-- Charles M. Schwab  (1862 – 1939)
American Steel Magnate

*Obstacles are those frightful things you see when you take your eyes off your goal.*
-- Henry Ford  (1863 – 1947)
American Business Magnate

*Go confidently in the direction of your dreams. Live the life you have imagined.*
-- Henry David Thoreau  (1817 – 1862)
American Philosopher & Abolitionist

*Life is a succession of lessons which must be lived to be understood.*
-- Helen Keller  (1880 – 1968)
American Author, Activist & Lecturer

*Expect problems and eat them for breakfast.*
-- Alfred A. Montapert  (1906 – 1997)
American Philosopher & Author

*When written in Chinese the word "crisis" is composed of two*
*characters – one represents danger*
*and the other represents opportunity.*
-- John F. Kennedy  (1917 – 1963)
35th President of the United States

**Tip:**  The ability to triumph begins not with where you came from, but with you.

Bonus Rust Buster #16
## Frolickingly Fresh Perspectives

Don't let a Discourager's negativity creep into *your* thoughts. Remember, they are looking for the worst possible outcomes.

Whether they merely relish playing devil's advocate to torment you or test your resolve or are jealous of your potential matters little.  We need to recognize that they have aesthetically challenged attitudes.  Okay, they may have ugly attitudes!  They may be just plain mean.

## Stinking Thinking is contagious.

We do not want to catch it.  To stay positive in the face of adversity is no easy task.  Surrounding ourselves with Encouragers and becoming more encouraging ourselves is most important.

We can also find great insulation from Discouragers in humor. A couple of earlier Rust Busters touched on the importance of a good sense of humor and the ability to laugh freely.  But creating a good humor habit requires some attention all its own.

Our 16th Rust Buster is all about laughter.  So here is more magic and mayhem… madness and meaning.

> *An optimist laughs to forget.  A pessimist forgets to laugh.*
> -- Tom Nansbury
> Also credited to: Tom Bodett (1955 -  )
> American Author & Actor

*As soap is to the body, so laughter is to the soul.*
— Jewish Proverb


*Keep a sense of humor. It doesn't mean you have to tell jokes.*
*If you can't think of anything else, when you're my age,*
*take off your clothes and walk in front of a mirror.*
*I guarantee you'll get a laugh.*
— Art Linkletter (1912 – 2010)
Canadian-American Media Personality


*At the height of laughter,*
*the universe is flung into a kaleidoscope of new possibilities.*
— Jean Houston (1937 - )
American Author


*Earth laughs in flowers.*
— Ralph Waldo Emerson (1803 – 1882)
American Poet, Lecturer & Philosopher


*Even the gods love jokes.*
— Plato (c428 – c384 BC)
Greek Philosopher


*From there to here, from here to there, funny things are everywhere.*
— Dr. Seuss (Pen Name)
Theodor Seuss Geisel (1904 – 1991)
American Author, Animator & Cartoonist

*A smile is the curve that sets everything straight.*
-- Phyllis Diller  (1917 – 2012)
American Comedian & Actress


*He who laughs, lasts!*
— Mary Pettibone Poole  (1938 -  )
American Author


*I was irrevocably betrothed to laughter, the sound of which has
always seemed to me to be the most civilized music in the world.*
— Peter Ustinov  (1921 – 2004)
English Actor, Writer & Filmmaker


*If you are happy and people around you are not happy, they will not
allow you to stay happy. Therefore, much of our happiness depends
upon our ability to spread happiness around us.*
– Dr. Madan Kataria  (1955 -  )
Founder of Laughter Yoga Movement


*Crying and laughing are the same emotion.
If you laugh too hard, you cry. And vice versa.*
— Sid Caesar  (1922 – 2014)
American Comic Actor


*If you don't learn to laugh at trouble,
you won't have anything to laugh at when you're old.*
— Edgar Watson Howe  (1853 – 1937)
American Novelist & Editor

*He that is of a merry heart has a continual feast.*
— Proverbs 15:15

*A well-balanced person is one*
*who finds both sides of an issue laughable.*
-- Herbert Prochnow  (1897 – 1998)
American Author & Toastmaster

*Laughter connects you with people.*
*It's almost impossible to maintain any kind of distance*
*or any sense of social hierarchy*
*when you're just howling with laughter.*
*Laughter is a force for democracy.*
— John Cleese  (1939 -  )
English Actor, Comedian & Producer

*Laughter has no foreign accent.*
— Paul Lowney  (1917 – 2007)
American Author & Humorist

*Laughter is a sense of proportion*
*and a power of seeing yourself from the outside.*
— Zero Mostel (1915 – 1977)
American Actor, Singer & Comedian

*Laughter is the corrective force*
*which prevents us from becoming cranks.*
— Henri-Louis Bergson (1859 – 1941)
French-Jewish Philosopher

*Against the assault of laughter,*
*nothing can stand.*
-- Mark Twain (Pen Name)
Samuel Clemens (1835 – 1910)
American Writer, Humorist & Lecturer


*Laughter is an instant vacation.*
-- Milton Berle (1908 – 2002)
American Comedian & Actor


*Laughter is the shortest distance between two people.*
— Victor Borge (Professional Name)
Børge Rosenbaum (1909 – 2000)
Danish-American Comedian & Pianist


*Laughter is the sun that drives winter from the human face.*
— Victor Hugo (1802 – 1885)
French Poet, Novelist & Dramatist


*Let us not use bombs and guns to overcome the world.*
*Let us use love and compassion.*
*Peace begins with a smile –*
*smile five times a day at someone you don't really want to smile at*
*– do it for peace.*
*So, let us radiate peace…and extinguish in the world and in the*
*hearts of all men all hatred and love for power.*
— Mother Teresa (1910 – 1997)
Albanian-Indian Nun & Missionary

*No matter what your heartache may be,*
*laughing helps you forget it for a few seconds.*
— Red Skelton (1913 – 1997)
American Comedian, Entertainer & Artist

*I love people who make me laugh.*
-- Audrey Hepburn (1929 – 1993)
British Actress, Dancer & Humanitarian

*Among those whom I like or admire,*
*I can find no common denominator.*
*But among those whom I love, I can.*
*All of them make me laugh.*
-- W. H. Auden (1907 – 1973)
English-American Poet

*Smiles are the soul's kisses.*
— Minna Thomas Antrim (1861 – 1950)
American Writer

*The art of medicine consists of amusing the patient*
*while nature cures the disease.*
— Voltaire (Pen Name)
François-Marie Arouet (1694 – 1778)
French Writer, Historian & Philosopher

*The best way to cheer yourself is to try to cheer someone else up.*
-- Mark Twain (Pen Name)
Samuel Clemens (1835 – 1910)
American Writer, Humorist & Lecturer

*The most wasted of all days is one without laughter.*
— E. E. Cummings (1894 – 1962)
American Poet, Author & Playwright


*The person who can bring the spirit of laughter into a room
is indeed blessed.*
— Bennett Cerf  (1898 – 1971)
American Publisher


*The young man who has not wept is a savage,
and the old man who will not laugh is a fool.*
— George Santayana (1863 – 1952)
Spanish-American Philosopher & Writer


*Those who do not know how to weep with their whole heart
don't know how to laugh either.*
— Golda Meir (1898 – 1978)
Israeli Teacher & Stateswoman
4th Prime Minister of Israel


*To truly laugh,
you must be able to take your pain and play with it.*
— Charlie Chaplin (1889 – 1977)
English Actor & Filmmaker


*Trouble knocked at the door, but,
hearing laughter, hurried away.*
— Benjamin Franklin (1706 – 1790)
American Author, Scientist & Diplomat
U.S.A. Founding Father

*True humor springs more from the heart than from the head;*
*it is not contempt, its essence is love.*
— Thomas Carlyle (1795 – 1881)
Scottish Philosopher & Writer

*We are all here for a spell.*
*Get all the good laughs you can.*
— Will Rogers (1879 – 1935)
American Actor, Cowboy & Humorist

*We don't laugh because we're happy,*
*we are happy because we laugh.*
— William James (1842 – 1910)
American Philosopher & Psychologist

*When humor goes, there goes civilization.*
— Erma Bombeck (1927 – 1996)
American Humorist & Writer

*When you realize how perfect everything is*
*you will tilt your head back and laugh at the sky.*
— Buddha  (c563 – c483 BC)
Founder of Buddhism

*With mirth and laughter let old wrinkles come.*
— William Shakespeare (1564 – 1616)
English Poet, Playwright & Actor

*You don't stop laughing because you grow old.*
*You grow old because you stop laughing.*
— George Bernard Shaw  (1856 - 1950)
Irish Playwright, Critic & Activist


*Your body cannot heal without play.*
*Your mind cannot heal without laughter.*
*Your soul cannot heal without joy.*
-- Catherine Fenwick
Canadian Author, Educator & Therapist


*A person who knows how to laugh at himself*
*will never cease to be amused.*
-- Shirley MacLaine (1934 -  )
American Actress


*A day without laughter is a day wasted.*
-- Charlie Chaplin  (1889 – 1977)
English Actor & Filmmaker


*If you're too busy to laugh, you are too busy.*
-- Proverb


*I don't trust anyone who doesn't laugh.*
-- Maya Angelou  (1928 – 2014)
American Poet & Civil Rights Activist

*You can't deny laughter;*
*when it comes,*
*it plops down in your favorite chair*
*and stays as long as it wants.*
-- Stephen King  (1947 -  )
American Author


*The human race has only one really effective weapon*
*and that is laughter.*
-- Mark Twain  (Pen Name)
Samuel Clemens  (1835 – 1910)
American Writer, Humorist & Lecturer


*It is cheerful to God*
*when you rejoice or laugh from the bottom of your heart.*
-- Martin Luther King, Jr.  (1929 – 1968)
American Minister & Civil Rights Activist


*When you have confidence,*
*you can have a lot of fun.*
*And when you have fun,*
*you can do amazing things.*
-- Joe Namath  (1943 -  )
American NFL Quarterback


**Tip:**  Encouragers love to laugh.  Share and celebrate encouragement and laughter with everyone you know.

## About the Author

Cathy Burnham Martin's first published work was at age 6, when an early poem won a town library contest. That was back when her parents refused to let her have the then-popular Chatty Cathy doll, stating that one chatty Cathy in the house was more than enough. Though poetry took a back seat, she has driven her writing and blabbing proficiencies along a highly eclectic career path through recruiting college students, corporate communications for a telecommunications company, TV broadcasting as News Anchor with an ABC affiliate, station management for an award-winning PEG access station, and bank organizing as Investor Relations Officer and Senior Vice President of Marketing. An active board member and volunteer, she received Easter Seals' David P. Goodwin Lifetime Commitment Award.

This professional voiceover artist, humorist, corporate communications geek, musical actress, journalist, and dedicated foodie earned numerous awards as a television news anchor and business woman. She has written, produced, and hosted groundbreaking documentaries, TV specials, and news reports, from the Moscow Super Power Summit and the opening of the Berlin Wall to coverage of New Hampshire's First-in-the-Nation Presidential Primaries.

A born storyteller and business speaker, Cathy is a member of the Actors Equity Association and a media coach. A 20-year Professional Member of the National Speakers Association, she continues speaking and coaching through SpeakEasy Corporate Communications.

Cathy Burnham Martin narrates her books as well as those of other authors. Audiobooks appear on such sites as Audible.com and Amazon. In addition to fiction and nonfiction books, Cathy writes articles for the GoodLiving123.com website.

www.ingramcontent.com/pod-product-compliance
Lightning Source LLC
LaVergne TN
LVHW051247080426
835513LV00016B/1788